THESE EXALTED ACRES

Unlocking the Secrets of Albany Rural Cemetery

BY PAUL GRONDAHL

PHOTOGRAPHY BY WILL WALDRON

A TIMES UNION PUBLICATION

THESE EXALTED ACRES

Unlocking the Secrets of Albany Rural Cemetery

BY PAUL GRONDAHL

PHOTOGRAPHY BY WILL WALDRON

Portions of this book, along with additional photography and videography, are available at http://timesunion.com/albanyrural. Join the conversation by adding your stories and reminiscences to the Web presentation.

Times Union
P.O. Box 15000
645 Albany Shaker Road
Albany, New York 12212

ISBN 978-0-578-13454-3

A TIMES UNION PUBLICATION

A LETTER FROM
ALBANY RURAL CEMETERY

AS you walk, run, bike or drive through the 467 acres of Albany Rural Cemetery, you see a beautiful landscape that is a monument to the rich legacy of our region. With the publication of this book and the series of articles in the Times Union, on timesunion.com and on the cemetery's website, the current stewards of Albany Rural thank all involved in this milestone project and encourage the continued engagement with this venerable institution.

A view from the South Ridge.

Incorporated in 1841, Albany Rural and its history are a fascinating tale of the social and cultural life of our region as well as a testament to environmental planning and care. Where else could you find such a congregation of politicians, scoundrels, artists, religious and social leaders and military heroes in the midst of a huge park and arboretum?

We are fortunate to have many people to thank for their leadership and support.

First, Chet Opalka as prime mover, philanthropist and gatherer of interested parties and talent. Additional key supporters include Karen Opalka, Doris P. Fischer, Richard J. Miller Jr. and Carol E.R. Miller, Christine Standish and the Standish Family Foundation, E. Stewart Jones, and Frank Slingerland, along with the over-arching interest and support of George R. Hearst III and the Times Union.

We invite you to join with us in celebrating this hallowed ground by visiting often, by taking part in tours and other programs, and by supporting it through membership and other contributions to secure its future for generations to come.

Sincerely,

Harry P. Meislahn

Harry P. Meislahn, president
Board of Directors
Albany Rural Cemetery

Officers: Frank M. Slingerland, vice president; Herbert G. Chorbajian, treasurer; and Anthony S. Esposito, secretary

Trustees: David E. Blabey, Willard A. Bruce, Jeffery Budrow, Audrey Hawkins, Michael Huxley, Jay Harold Jakovic, E. Stewart Jones, Carolyn Snyder Lemmon, Doris Fischer Malesardi, John S. Pipkin, Michael S. Radlick, Norman S. Rice and Josey Twombly

ALBANY RURAL CEMETERY

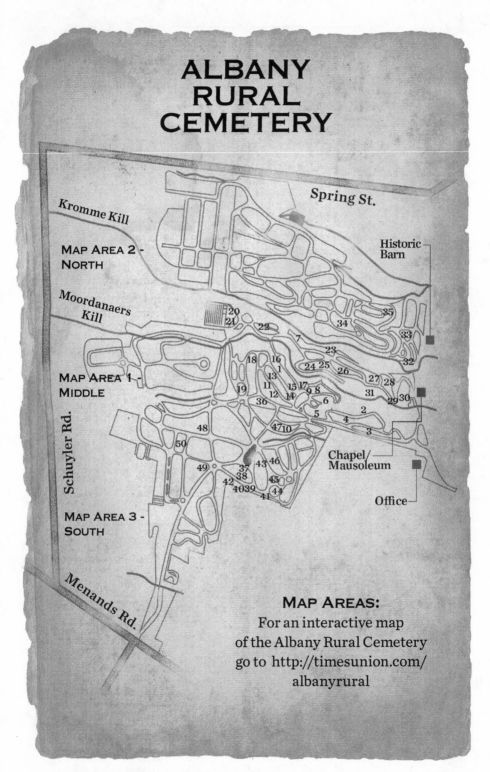

Spring St.

Kromme Kill

Moordanaers Kill

Schuyler Rd.

Menands Rd.

MAP AREA 2 - NORTH

MAP AREA 1 - MIDDLE

MAP AREA 3 - SOUTH

Historic Barn

Chapel/ Mausoleum

Office

MAP AREAS:
For an interactive map of the Albany Rural Cemetery go to http://timesunion.com/ albanyrural

CONTENTS

FOREWORD

Albany Rural Cemetery, incorporated in 1841, is one of the oldest and grandest examples of the rural cemetery movement in America. Historians come from around the country and overseas to walk its 467 acres, to study its stately monuments and to savor its parklike setting. It earned a spot on the National Register of Historic Places.

More than 135,000 people are buried here. It is an epic city of the dead, a history lesson carved in stone.

In the Victorian era, hundreds toured its grounds by horse-drawn carriage each weekend to honor the deceased. Annual subscription books were sold.

Today, Albany Rural is an overlooked gem. It is one of the region's great cultural resources and it deserves a deeper appreciation. The silent, sprawling grounds beckon, an invitation of solitude and sustenance for the soul.

INTRODUCTION

Dead leaves crackled underfoot as Michael and Lynn Radlick jogged through Albany Rural Cemetery in the half-light of an October morning, their before-work ritual for the past 20 years.

A gauzy dawn slowly illuminated stark gray granite obelisks and ornate white marble monuments that seemed to hover above wreaths of mist and fog in hollows and swales.

It was a dreamlike scene, unmoored from time and space. On this moody fall morning in 2013, these 467 acres, this great city of the dead, could have been mistaken for an idyllic tableau in 1883.

"We start our run on a busy road, and it feels like we're going back in time when we get into the cemetery, because it's so peaceful and quiet," said Michael Radlick, a cemetery trustee who is working on a book about its history with an emphasis on designer David Bates Douglass. The couple has boxes of historical material, and they've taken thousands of photographs of the cemetery in all seasons.

"There's always something new and beautiful to see here," said Lynn Radlick, who has relatives buried here. "It's a graveyard, but I really see it as a place where we come to celebrate life."

There is a timeless quality to Albany Rural Cemetery. It is a parkland with 35 miles of

Michael and Lynn Radlick enjoy an early morning run on South Ridge Road.

pathways. It is a nature preserve, open-air art museum, architectural primer, history classroom and genealogy archive. Incorporated April 2, 1841, it is listed on the National Register of Historic Places and represents one of the earliest and grandest examples of the rural cemetery movement in America.

Today, Albany Rural Cemetery seems a hidden secret of the Capital Region, reflecting, among other things, the way in which contemporary society has outsourced death.

The cemetery's office staff is asked on a weekly basis if they still do burials. They are open for business, averaging 170 interments each year, with plenty of room for additional plots. Cremation services also are offered at the public, not-for-profit, nonsectarian cemetery run by a board of trustees, the Albany Cemetery Association. The religiously affiliated Saint Agnes Ceme-

tery and Beth Emeth Cemetery adjoin it.

Although it has lost its place of cultural prominence in recent times, Albany Rural Cemetery is, numerically speaking, the most populous city in the region.

It is the final resting place of 55 mayors of Albany, five governors, 34 members of Congress, eight presidential Cabinet members and one president, Chester Alan Arthur, whose plot is the most frequently visited.

And that's just the politicians. Iron magnates and railroad barons, quintessential American success stories and black sheep of illustrious families are buried here. Exultation and heartbreak are woven through the threads of heroic and tragic narratives that knit the disparate stories of those laid to rest in these rolling acres.

"It's rewarding to help people in their time of need,"

said general manager John Buszta, who has worked at the cemetery for 34 years and oversees a staff of 14. Albany Rural has managed to break even in recent years on an annual budget of roughly $800,000, while maintaining an endowment of a few million dollars.

But it faces increased competition, particularly from the 351-acre Gerald B.H. Solomon Saratoga National Cemetery in Schuylerville, founded in 1999, which offers free burials for veterans and eligible dependents.

Today, the average cost of a single burial plot at Albany Rural Cemetery is $900. Subscription books for lots in the newly incorporated and landscaped Albany Rural were opened in June 1845, and people who made the highest bids were entitled to first choice. The bids for lots ranged from $1 to $80, with an average price of $25 for a 16-foot-by-16-foot parcel.

More than 135,000 documented burials have taken place over the past 172 years. The remains of thousands more Colonial-era residents of Albany — slaves and their wealthy owners, Dutch dowagers and risk-taking young colonists felled by disease — were dug up in 1868 from the State Street burial grounds along Washington Park in Albany and re-interred en masse on Albany Rural's northwestern edge. No map shows who went where.

Visitors to the cemetery can read a backstory in Victorian-era symbolism and carved iconography that is repeated across the sprawling grounds in a kind of cultural short-

The grave of President Chester Alan Arthur. (Page 54)

hand: a torch inverted for a life extinguished; oak leaves and an acorn for a person of old age; ivy for friendship and fidelity; and crossed swords for a life lost in battle.

It is a monumental mirror held up to the region's past, and sometimes the heavy weight of history is almost too much to bear. We can trace the ancient heartache of scores of infants and young mothers who died in childbirth in the 1800s. There are vestigial reminders of successive waves of long-conquered diseases such as typhoid, yellow fever, cholera and influenza that killed many Albany citizens. The toll of the nation's wars are commemorated here, too, from the Revolutionary War to 1,030 Civil War soldiers and sailors buried at Albany Rural, as well as casualties of World War I and World War II.

Notes of triumph temper the sadness, too, with monuments that celebrate great industrialists, inventors, entrepreneurs, educators and other successful individuals.

The tumult of the human condition is carved in outsized

funerary objects that bring to mind the tantalizing title of William Kennedy's narrative of the city's history: "O Albany! Improbable City of Political Wizards, Fearless Ethnics, Spectacular Aristocrats, Splendid Nobodies, and Underrated Scoundrels."

The landscape appealed to filmmaker Hector Babenco, who shot scenes of his vision of Kennedy's novel, "Ironweed," a redemption tale about Depression-era bums, in Albany Rural.

*****

There was a time when it was not a foreign country of past tense. At its peak in the late-19th century, Albany Rural Cemetery was as popular as a Victorian theme park. Annual subscription tickets were sold. Thick guidebooks and picture postcards were printed. Romantic poems and hymns were dedicated to its sylvan beauty.

"What a refuge shall it be, from shivering misery, and squalid want, from secret griefs, from penury, oppression, injustice — in short, from the world," D.D. Barnard said in his address at the cemetery's epic consecration ceremony Oct. 7, 1844, attended by thousands who arrived by horse-drawn carriages and stayed for a four-hour program of music, speeches and ceremony.

For decades after, trains from Albany ran on the hour and disgorged hundreds of passengers on languid Saturday afternoons in spring, summer and fall. Men in three-piece suits and top hats walked arm-in-arm with women in bustle skirts, twirling parasols. Children in knickers and crinoline scampered ahead and raced through the graceful, classical stone gate on Broadway designed by Marcus T. Reynolds, architect of the D&H Building and a half-dozen other landmarks in Albany, as well as several of the most impressive monuments in the cemetery.

Columns of picnickers, day trippers and mourners intent on visiting family burial plots climbed into horse-drawn wagons and clopped up the dirt path beneath a canopy of overhanging shade trees, the start of a two-hour, eight-mile grand tour of the cemetery.

The tour began just off Broadway at the office, known as the Lodge, a striking red sandstone building by Robert W. Gibson built in 1882 in a Gothic Revival style reminiscent of his best-known design, the Cathedral of All Saints in Albany. Gibson put his Gothic stamp on the 1884 chapel, just up the road from his Lodge and clad in the same distinctive sandstone, Potsdam red.

Reynolds also designed the nearby superintendent's

Marcus T. Reynolds, c. 1897, architect of many structures throughout the cemetery. (Page 44).

house, a quietly graceful and shingled Colonial gem built in 1899.

They thronged here a century ago to honor the dead, but also to rubber-neck over the tasteful architectural grandeur commissioned by the old money of Albany's ancient Dutch and English families: the Van Rensselaers, Pruyns, Lansings, Cornings, et al. Just as the rich lived close to each other in the city's exclusive neighborhoods centuries ago, they were buried together in close proximity, and their imposing monuments still advertise their Gilded Age wealth and prestige.

Albany Rural Cemetery is a garden of delights whose devotees are drawn to its inspiring vastness for a variety of reasons.

The Radlicks combine all-season exercise with a fascination for long-lost architectural relics — tumbledown stone bridges, wrought-iron fences, shards of Victorian-era benches — that litter remote areas of the ravines rarely visited now. Six lost lakes formed by dams

on the two streams were removed decades ago, due to concerns over erosion, The lakes were drained around the time carriages and trolleys stopped taking visitors on public tours.

The couple and others like them — dog walkers, joggers, history buffs, birdwatchers, photographers, out-of-town tourists and, of course, descendants of those buried — have begun to reclaim Albany Rural as a peaceful locale of reflection and recreation.

"I love this place and have come to think of it as a sanctuary," Michael Radlick said. "The more you explore the cemetery and learn its history, the more excited you get about it."

*****

The creation of Albany Rural Cemetery grew out a sense of communal guilt. There was a time in the early years of a young republic striving to survive and prosper when America's dead were an overlooked and neglected constituency.

"The living were doing well enough; it is time to think of the dead," wrote a group of Albany's prominent citizens who met Dec. 30, 1840, in the YMCA room of the Exchange Building at State Street and Broadway. City commerce had hit a record high that year, and newfound prosperity led business leaders to "take into account the importance of purchasing a plat of ground for a new public cemetery."

Its planning was spurred by a rising outcry over perceived threats to public health from tainted water and contagious disease from a large, overcrowded urban burying ground on State Street along today's Washington Park. Before that, several churchyard cemeteries downtown had run out of space, with coffins buried three or four deep, and sometimes they washed away after spring floods.

In a sermon delivered in December 1840, the Rev. Bartholomew T. Welch, pastor of Emmanuel Baptist Church, railed against the "wholly inexcusable" condition of the city's graveyards. He lamented that "for 150 years the city's dead had found no abiding rest."

The Industrial Revolution was churning at full throttle. The factories and mills choked city residents with soot and grime. Transplanted farmers who poured into the cities to find work harbored a nostalgia for the serene countryside they had left behind.

These broad trends converged in the rural cemetery movement that began with Mount Auburn in Cambridge, Mass., in 1831; Laurel Hill in Philadelphia in 1836; and Green-Wood in Brooklyn in 1838 — the latter also designed by Douglass.

In 1841, Albany Rural stepped into the vanguard of the national movement that featured classical monuments in rolling landscaped terrain that was parklike. These peaceful, naturally beautiful grounds — privately owned and operated — were designed to reflect a romantic, Victorian-era view of death. It marked a distinct break from church-affiliated graveyards in the Colonial era, and the movement appropriated a Greek word, *koimeterion*, or cemetery, which means "a

The view from the top of Middle Ridge Road looking east toward Troy.

sleeping place."

In Albany, organizers considered the names of "The Evergreens" and "Tawasentha" before Albany Rural Cemetery was settled on. A location across the Hudson River, in East Greenbush, Rensselaer County, was examined before the site in Menands now bordered by Route 378 and Broadway was chosen.

The Douglass design at Albany Rural features broad sloping lawns, miles of labyrinthine roads and pathways, a limpid pool, shaded ravines, two streams, a picturesque waterfall and hundreds of beautiful shade trees. There were once seven lakes created by building dams on the two streams, Moordanaers Kill and Kromme Kill, that meander through Albany Rural, and they were christened with idyllic names such as Tawasentha, Bethesda and Consecration Lake.

The popularity of the rural cemetery movement inspired an offshoot movement, the creation of large public parks in urban areas, including 90-acre Washington Park in Albany, which opened to the public in 1871.

Washington Park borrowed a similar concept of classical monuments scattered across carefully landscaped grounds by transforming the city's former parade ground and the old graveyard, after remains were moved to Albany Rural Cemetery in 1868.

"Albany Rural Cemetery is as large and impressive as any of the rural cemeteries, including Green-Wood, but local recognition is abysmal," said John Pipkin, a cemetery trustee and a professor of geography at the University at Albany, who specializes in urbanism. He started visiting the cemetery in the 1990s at the urging of Norman Rice, the longest-tenured trustee.

"It's about the illusion of blending together nouveau riche and old wealth and a Whig version of social class," Pipkin said. "The great dichotomy here is between the 1 percent and the 99 percent."

Other intrigues defy classification, and the cemetery attracts its share of devotees of the mystical, who say they have discovered in its shrouded acres signs of the occult. There are mysteries with an equally elusive explanation, such as the bouquet of fresh-cut flowers placed in the hands of an angel at a monument to the Lathrop sisters: children's book illustrator Dorothy and sculptor Gertrude. The flowers appeared regularly over the course of 20 years, but nobody ever saw who placed them there. And a fresh half-grapefruit was left for many years atop the Walter Fredenburgh monument. Lore had it that the man's widow, who had cut him a fresh grapefruit every morning for breakfast, had devised the citrus memorial. At the plot of the prominent Pruyn family, someone sporadically placed uncooked broccoli and potatoes atop the markers, the significance of which continues to baffle.

*****

Today, Albany Rural remains a beguiling blend of the natural and the manmade. The grounds sprout with sandstone, marble and granite carved with names and dates of the city's powerful and prosperous, and history's relentless march. The cemetery also is a 19th-century engineering marvel, with utility pole-sized obelisks and sarcophagi as big as automobiles hewn in a single mass out of the ground between Albany and New Hampshire. There are Parthenon-inspired mausoleums assembled one-ton block by one-ton block. These stony behemoths were carried by train or barge to sprawling stone works that lined the cemetery grounds a century ago. Inside cold and drafty warehouses, dozens of stone carvers bent over their dusty, back-breaking toil as the metallic song of hammer and

The Lathrop burial site angel sculpture for Dorothy and Gertrude Lathrop. (Page 33)

chisel rang out through heavy air choked with stone dust.

It was a small-scale local version of the construction of the pyramids of ancient Egypt. The heaviest and biggest monuments and obelisks were carved and set aside for winter, when they were hauled more easily over the snow-covered frozen acres by teams of oxen or draft horses, hoisted into place by rope and pulley and the brawn of a dozen laborers.

"I had no interest in cemeteries. I blame our dog," said Michael Huxley, a cemetery trustee and former science administrator for the Smithsonian Institution. He has become an expert on the stone carvers and stone works of a century ago and he tracked "my carvers" across the Northeast and beyond during research forays to more than 100 cemeteries. His wife, Carole, began walking their Jack Russell terrier, Gregan, through the cemetery each morning starting 15 years ago. Huxley took the after-

noon dog-walk shift. As the dog grew older and his pace slowed, Huxley found he had plenty of time to scrutinize the monuments. He began seeing the names of certain carvers who proudly signed their handiwork on numerous memorials. It piqued his scholarly interest. A research avocation was born. After Gregan died, the Huxleys continued the twice-daily walks with their new dog, Archie, a terrier mix.

"We're so lucky, because dogs are forbidden in a lot of cemeteries," he said. "Albany Rural Cemetery's trustees were smart. Dog walkers spend a lot of time in the cemetery, and they discourage vandalism and theft."

*****

Some made mockery of the term "final resting place." For example, Revolutionary War hero Gen. Philip Schuyler was moved at least three times before his remains were interred at Albany Rural Cemetery in the late 1800s. That was more than a century after he won glory as a commander at the Battle of Saratoga, a turning point in the American Revolution.

He also was the father-in-law of Founding Father Alexander Hamilton — Hamilton married Schuyler's daughter Elizabeth on Dec. 14, 1780, in the parlor of the Schuyler mansion in the city's South End.

Alas, today nobody is quite certain where the famous general is buried, since some cemetery records stored in a downtown Albany bank went missing decades ago and the old Dutch families did not always bother with paperwork when it came to a privately owned family burial plot. As far as anyone can tell, Schuyler's bones wound up in the Van Rensselaer family plot, relatives through marriage, and not beneath a 50-foot polished granite column his descendants erected as a memorial to him in another part of the cemetery.

Century-old maps of the cemetery depict a ghostly line, a stairway, leading to an underground vault on the Van Rensselaer plot. But the stairway was long ago covered over with topsoil and grass. Now it would take permission of descendants of the Van Rensselaers to excavate the site in order to get to the bottom of the mystery.

"I think it could be like King Tut's tomb," Norman Rice said with a cackle, waving his arms in delight over the thought of such a modern-day spectacle. He has floated the idea past a few of the descendants of Stephen Van Rensselaer, the last patroon, and they said they would consider it.

Rice knows as much about the cemetery, its people, its history and its intrigues as anyone alive. For decades, he led popular walking tours of the cemetery, three-hour marathons laced with his extraordinary command of Albany's history and sprinkled with juicy tidbits of gossip gleaned from friendships with many of the descendants of the storied families who populate Albany Rural Cemetery.

Rice is emeritus director of the Albany Institute of History & Art and, at 88 years old, he walks haltingly and with the aid of a cane these days. But the years melt away when

Albany historian Norman Rice, emeritus director of the Albany Institute of History & Art.

he drives out into the cemetery and pauses at the plots of the city's grand patriarchs like Erastus Corning or John Boyd Thacher or William James.

"For historians, this is the promised land," Rice said. He was standing in the center of the brooding and evocative James family plot, near the monument to patriarch William James, one of the wealthiest people in 19th-century Albany. He was the grandfather of the famous writer Henry James and influential philosopher William James. Rice raised his cane and pointed out the adjacent monuments to the fabulous Reynolds brothers, architect Marcus T. and historian Cuyler. Also nearby is the stunning Lathrop obelisk topped by a Greek goddess, created by Jane Lathrop Stanford and her husband, Leland, a railroad magnate and co-founder of Stanford University. A neighboring plot is dominated by the granite sarcophagus of Ira Harris, judge and U.S. senator and friend of Abra-

ham Lincoln, whose sister, Phoebe Harris Phelps, was a victim of horrific domestic violence. His daughter, Clara Harris, and his future son-in-law, Henry Rathbone, were the Lincolns' guests at Ford's Theatre on April 14, 1865, when the president was shot and killed by John Wilkes Booth. The grim and bloody tragedy haunted the couple, whose tortured lives ended in madness and murder.

*****

Rice may yet crack the mystery of the Van Rensselaer vault, but this ancient city of stone is slow to yield its secrets.

Those who know its grounds with great authority, and there are only a handful, have spent decades prowling its monumental acres and an equal amount of time scouring archives and reading history books to parse out the extraordinary people and their remarkable stories.

Nobody has dug more deeply into the lives of the

people buried there than Peter Hess, former president of the cemetery board. He published three books of short biographies of notables buried at Albany Rural, wrote dozens of articles on the cemetery's people and history for its newsletter and led public tours for many years. He blames Rice for his interest.

Hess bought Albany Steel in 1985. The Menands business is adjacent to Albany Rural Cemetery and he started jogging through its winding roadways and exploring its sprawling acres. Rice encouraged his study and took Hess to an Albany rare book dealer. He also suggested numerous reference books that could aid his research. The self-taught historian has only scratched the surface after a three-decade labor of love.

"This area doesn't get the credit it deserves," Hess said. "Albany is the oldest continuously occupied settlement in the 13 colonies. The people buried here are absolutely amazing. They fought and won the Revolutionary War, drafted the Constitution, built major corporations and became leaders in industry. Albany Rural Cemetery is one of the most historic places in all of New York state and even the country. Unfortunately, it remains under-appreciated."

Hess is drawn to the city's founding fathers, and one of his all-time favorites is Robert Yates, a delegate to the first U.S. Constitutional Convention and a leading anti-Federalist. But he also has met more-contemporary characters in the cemetery, includ-

Peter Hess, former Albany Rural Cemetery board president, at the grave site of Robert Yates, a leading patriot. (Page 28)

ing notorious resident Gary Evans. The antiques thief, sociopath and murderer who confessed to killing five men, lived in a makeshift camp in the cemetery's ravines and looted several historic items, including a 1,000-pound carved stone bench, which he fenced for cash with antiques dealers.

"I come here to relax," Evans told Hess. "I find it very peaceful."

"We know you're here stealing," Hess said.

Years after Evans died jumping off the Troy-Menands Bridge to escape the law in 1998, Hess discovered that Evans had scratched his name on the back of a tombstone and carved into another grave marker a short poem, similar to verses he scrawled on a suicide note: "I'm going to a place where the sun shines brighter and the stars are always out."

*****

Stefan Bielinski began spending time at Albany Rural Cemetery in the early 1980s, around the time he started building the Colonial Albany Social History Project, a rich trove of linked websites with biographies of dozens of 17th-, 18th- and 19th-century residents of Albany. To him, they are "my people."

"I came here looking for my people, which is the history of the inarticulate," said Bielinski, a retired State Museum social historian. "Albany Rural is a great place to trace the lives of people from Colonial Albany."

In particular, he studied the faint historical record of slaves and free people of color, which led him to discover the family plot of Samuel Schuyler, a ship captain and the wealthy patriarch of the so-called "black Schuylers," whose large monument and family plot is located in a prime location among wealthy families of Dutch descent. His research also focused on another area of the cemetery, the Church Grounds, also known as the Corporation Plot, where the remains of thousands of Colonial-era residents were re-interred in 1868 from the burial grounds on Albany's State Street.

"I wanted to reclaim the humanity of these people," Bielinski said. "The black community deserves a history that includes more than mentions when they did something wrong. By tracing the genealogies of the black Schuylers and other early black settlers, I've been able to show the evolution of Albany's black middle class."

Bielinski was concerned about an ongoing, accelerated deterioration of the tombstones in the Church Grounds, where blacks who were members of the African Methodist Episcopal Church were shunted off to a corner section along the tree line, segregated as they were in the Albany graveyard. Bielinski has researched the lives of several slaves buried here, although their names and dates are slowly being erased from the fragile marble markers. The cemetery does not have the resources to take on a large-scale gravestone restoration and preservation project.

"The people of Colonial Albany deserve better," he said. "Albany in 1790 was a complex multiracial, multicultural city. There were 592 slaves in Albany in 1790 and half the households owned at least one slave. We can't leave the people of color out of the story of Albany. Otherwise, it's an incomplete story."

*****

Bill Bruce, a former commissioner of Albany's Department of General Services, has been hanging out in Albany

Stefan Bielinski, retired senior historian at the State Museum, stands next to the grave of Capt. Samuel Schuyler. (Page 72)

Rural Cemetery for more than 45 years, since he was a teenager who lived on Bacon Lane in Loudonville along the cemetery's northern border. In the summer of 1969, after returning from Woodstock, he romanced a girlfriend as they strolled its scenic acres and they had a favorite bench where they sat and kissed. He mowed lawns and worked on the grounds crew for a few summers while he attended Shaker High School. He came back after he and his wife married. When she was pregnant, they strolled through the monuments looking for baby names they liked.

"You couldn't help but fall in love with this place," Bruce said.

As Albany's general services commissioner, he was in charge of 60 city parks, including Washington Park, but none could compare to Albany Rural. "It's my favorite open space or park in the Capital Region," said Bruce, a trustee and former board president who has also written articles for the cemetery newsletter.

Bruce is of Scottish descent

and has done the bulk of his research on the notable Scots buried in the cemetery, including Archibald McIntyre, who operated a large iron ore mine and smelting operation in the Adirondacks. The family plot includes the graves of McIntyre's prominent sons-in-law, Dr. James McNaughton, a president of Albany Medical College, and David Henderson, who died in a hiking tragedy in the Adirondacks.

"You could spend your whole life researching the people buried in this cemetery," Bruce said. "Every time I come, I see something new and different."

*****

It has taken 20 years of dogged research for Mark Bodnar to track down the graves of 1,030 Civil War soldiers and sailors buried in Albany Rural Cemetery, including 26 generals, six Medal of Honor recipients and three Confederate soldiers. "It's a target-rich environment," said Bodnar, who worked for many years at the Watervliet Arsenal. "This was the right cemetery to do Civil War research."

He is president of the Historical Society of the town of Colonie and leads popular Civil War tours of the cemetery. He is also at work on a book on the topic. In addition to the 149 Union Army soldiers buried beside identical headstones in the Soldiers' Lot, created in 1862 by the federal government, among Bodnar's favorite graves are those of Charles Elliott Pease and William Henry Pohlmann.

Pease was an Albany shopkeeper's son and Union College graduate who joined Company G of 44th Infantry New York and carried a letter requesting terms of surrender from Gen. Robert E. Lee to Gen. Ulysses S. Grant on April 9, 1865. He rode with Grant that day to the Appomattox Court House and the adjacent Wilmer McLean house, the site agreed upon for the surrender. After the documents were signed, Grant ordered Pease to escort Lee back to his headquarters as a courtesy.

"It was an extraordinary assignment to ride with Grant and Lee on the same day, especially for a 27-year-old soldier from Albany," Bodnar said.

Bodnar can offer detailed commentary on dozens of soldiers, including Brig. Gen. James Clay Rice, a Civil War casualty, whose obelisk contains his final recorded words: "Turn me over and let me die with my face to the foe."

*****

For Norman Rice, the favorite time of day at Albany Rural Cemetery is just before dusk. The sun is low on the horizon and the oblique angle illuminates and sharpens faded

The Archibald McIntyre family grave. (Page 29)

carvings on gravestones and casts long, ominous shadows across monuments and mausoleums. Artists call it "the raking light."

The cemetery is normally deserted at that hour, shortly before the wrought-iron gates are locked for the night, and the raking light offers moody moments of portent that seem to stretch out, suspended between day and night, past and present.

Rice paused at his favorite spot, the Corning family plot, where patriarch Erastus Corning, founder of the New York Central Railroad, and five generations of Cornings are buried. The raking light cut across two people who were huddled around a necklace of seven identical stones in rose-hued granite.

Rice leaned on his cane and approached the pair.

Rice embraced Jamie Corning of Kansas City and her brother Ed Corning of Brunswick, who were visiting their family plot. They are a niece and nephew of Mayor Erastus Corning 2nd.

"This is remarkable," Rice said, his voice choked with

emotion. "I haven't seen you in more than 50 years, since you were little children running around the Corning Farm. I spent summers there, and those were the happiest days of my life."

They stood beneath the bare branches of a big cucumber magnolia tree planted long ago by the mayor's wife, Betty. They caught up on family matters and the storied history of the Cornings. Ed Corning told Rice about an oil painting of an ancestor and other archival material he had acquired. "I guess I'm the keeper of a very old flame," he said.

The light was almost gone now as they stood in the center of the plot of one of the most distinguished families Albany has produced. They hugged and said goodbye.

Rice was silent as he moved back to his car. Dusk had enveloped the cemetery. In the dying light, one could no longer make out the words carved into the monument of the patriarch's son, Erastus Corning Jr. It said: "Neither Shall There Be Any More Pain, For The Former Things Are Passed Away."

Carved Clues

Many old gravestones include carved details filled with symbolism. As you embark on a trip through Albany Rural Cemetery, here are some details to look for and some interpretations that can be drawn about the life of the person the stone memorializes:

ANCHOR: Hope, sometimes maritime or naval service; also early Christian symbol

ANGELS: Rebirth, resurrection, protection, judgment, wisdom, mercy

ARROW: Mortality

BALL OR ORB: Faith

BIBLE: Knowledge, sometimes deceased minister or teacher

BUGLE: Military service, the resurrection

BUTTERFLY: Short-lived, an early death

CANNON: Military service (when found on base of stone, might mean artillery)

CELTIC CROSS: Faith and eternity, often Irish ancestry

CHAIN WITH THREE LINKS: Trinity, faith, a symbol of the Odd Fellows

CHAIR, SMALL: Infant's chair, indicating death of child

CHERUB: Innocence, may mark grave of a child

COFFIN: Also tomb or sarcophagus. Mortality, mourning

COLUMN: Noble life

COLUMN, BROKEN: Head of family, early death, grief

COMPASS AND SQUARE: Uprightness, judgment, deceased usually a member of the Masons

CORN: Old age

Anchor

Finger pointing up

CROSS: Christian faith, resurrection

CROWN: Glory of life-after-death, with cross, may indicate Masonic membership

CUP OR CHALICE: The Christian sacrament

D.A.R.: Daughters of the American Revolution

DOLPHIN: Resurrection, salvation, bearer of souls across water to heaven

DOVE: Love, purity, resurrection, the holy spirit, often indicates death of child

EAGLE: Courage, faith, generosity, contemplation, military service

EYE: Humility, may indicate Masonic membership

FACE, WINGED: Effigy of the deceased soul, the soul in flight

FEMALE FIGURE: Sorrow, grief

FINGER POINTING UP: Pathway to heaven,

Chair, small

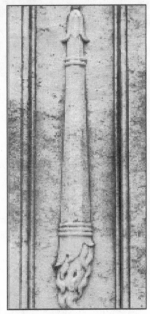

Torch inverted

heavenly reward

FISH: Faith, life, spiritual nourishment, gospel symbol; may indicate military service

FLYING BIRD: Rebirth

G.A.R.: Grand Army of the Republic, veteran of the Civil War; seen most often on metal flag holders

GARLAND: Victory over death

CARVED CLUES

GUN: Military service

HANDS CLASPED: Farewell hope of meeting in eternity, the everlasting union of husband and wife

HARP: Hope; may have broken string

HAT, CIVIL WAR-STYLED: The kepi worn by Civil War soldiers, indicates veteran

HELMET: Military service, strength, protection

HOURGLASS: With wings attached, represents shortness of life, mortality

IVY: Friendship, fidelity, affection and eternal life

LAMB: Innocence; may mark grave of a child

LAUREL: Fame, victory, triumph

LILY: Innocence and purity, sometimes chastity

LION: Courage, bravery, strength, symbol of St. Mark

LOTUS: Sleep, purity, resurrection, perfect beauty, spiritual revelation

MISTLETOE: Immortality

MOMENTO MORI: Carved inscription "remember death" in Latin, reminds viewer of mortality

MORNING GLORY: Beginning of life

MYRTLE: Undying love, peace

NAKED FIGURE: Truth, purity, innocence

OAK LEAVES AND ACORN: Maturity, old age

OBELISK: Four-sided tapered column, with pyramidal top. Symbolizes rebirth, connection between heaven and Earth. An Egyptian element, obelisks are sometimes topped with Christian cross

OLIVE BRANCH: Peace, forgiveness, humanity

OPEN GATES: Afterlife, the soul entering heaven

Hourglass

G.A.R.

Urn

OWL: Wisdom, solitude, a warning of impending death

PALM BRANCH: Victory and rejoicing

PANSY: Flower signifying remembrance, meditation

POPPY: Sleep, eternal sleep

PYRAMID: Resurrection, eternal life, enlightenment, spiritual attainment

RIFLE: Military service

RING, BROKEN: A family severed

ROSE: Flower signifying victory, pride, triumphant love, purity

ROSE IN FULL BLOOM: Prime of life

ROSEBUD: Morning of life

SHIELD: Indicates military service

SKULL: With crossed bones, transitory nature of earthly life, penitence, mortality

STAR: Divine guidance, many other meanings

SWORD: Military service (when found on base of stone might mean infantry)

SWORD INVERTED: Relinquishment of power, victory, military service

SWORD SHEATHED: Temperance, military service

SWORDS CROSSED: Life lost in battle

THISTLE: Scottish descent, earthly sorrow, defiance

TORCH: Immortality, purification, truth, wisdom

TORCH INVERTED: Life extinguished

TREE STUMP: Life interrupted

TREE TRUNK: Brevity of life, number of broken branches can indicate deceased family members at site

TRIANGLE: Holy trinity

URN: Immortality, penitence, death of the body and its return to dust in the final resting place

WEEPING WILLOW: Sorrow, mourning, lamentation, sometimes with urn

WHEAT SHEAF: Old age, fruitful life

WREATH: Victory

MIDDLE

ALBANY RURAL CEMETERY

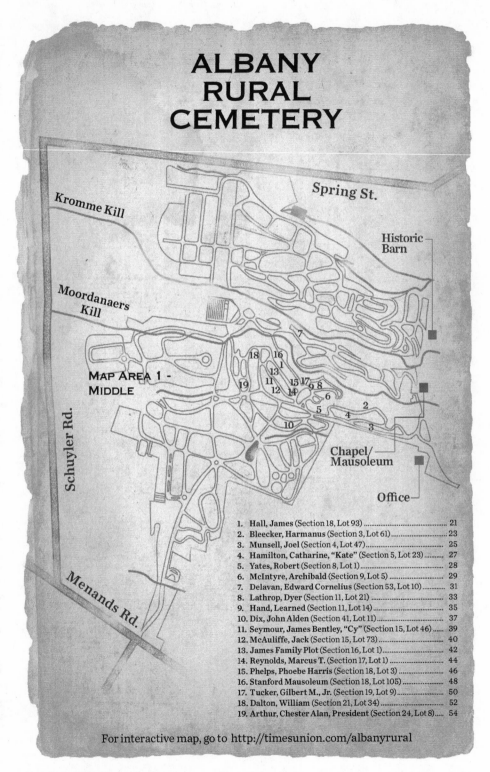

Spring St.

Kromme Kill

Moordanaers Kill

Historic Barn

MAP AREA 1 - MIDDLE

Schuyler Rd.

Chapel/ Mausoleum

Office

Menands Rd.

For interactive map, go to http://timesunion.com/albanyrural

James Hall
(1811-1898)

FATHER OF MODERN GEOLOGY,
FOUNDER OF THE NEW YORK STATE MUSEUM

J ames Hall was the pre-eminent geologist and paleontologist in 19th-century America. He founded the State Museum and served an unprecedented six decades, holding both positions of state geologist and paleontologist.

He visited the site himself when "some unknown beast" was discovered at Harmony Mills in Cohoes. He was responsible for bringing to the State Museum the Cohoes Mastodon in 1866. It became the museum's most popular draw and the institution's iconic specimen. It has been on display for 147 years.

Hall secured his legacy by publishing the seminal 13-volume masterwork, "The Paleontology of New York." Another lasting contribution was his work on the geosyncline concept of mountain-building, which found that sediment buildup in a shallow basin causes the basin to sink, simultaneously forcing the adjacent area to rise.

Hall was widely revered for his perennial battles with the state Legislature, and he argued vigorously for increasing funding for scientific research. His colleagues hailed him as a headstrong, single-minded and tenacious advocate of their work.

Hall was born in Hingham, Mass., the oldest of four children born to James Hall Sr. and Sousanna Dourdain Hall, who emigrated from England. He developed an early interest in nature and studied sea life in tidal inlets

James Hall was the New York State geologist and paleontologist. His grave is near the Stanford burial, (p.48), vault in Section 18.

JAMES HALL: (1811-1898)

Historical marker at the grave of James Hall highlights his vast career in geology.

and collected shells along the Massachusetts shore. He enrolled in the Rensselaer School in Troy (Rensselaer Polytechnic Institute today), and studied natural sciences under noted geologist Amos Eaton. Hall graduated with honors in 1832, earned a master's degree the next year and was hired as an assistant professor of chemistry and natural sciences at the school. In 1836, he was made full professor of geology. He did survey work for Stephen Van Rensselaer, the "last patroon" and founder of RPI.

He was hired for a four-year survey project funded by the state Legislature that collected information on the geology and natural history of New York. Hall was teamed with acclaimed geologist Ebenezer Em-

mons and he traversed the Adirondack Mountains and western New York, gathering fossils and many types of specimens.

At the conclusion of the survey in 1841, Hall had proven his skills and was named the first state geologist. He and his wife, Sarah, settled in Albany where he spent his entire career in state service.

In 1870, the New York State Museum of Natural History was created, and Hall was appointed its first director. In 1893, a law was passed that appointed Hall state geologist and paleontologist for life. He also published a massive and influential volume, "Geology of New York," which remains a classic work in the field.

Hall traveled to St.

Petersburg, Russia, at age 85 for the International Geological Congress and joined an expedition in the Ural Mountains. He died two years later. He is buried with his wife in Section 18, Lot 93, near the office, a short way up South Ridge Road.

A bronze plaque near a large, granite marker lists a few of Hall's career highlights: co-founder and first president of the Geological Society of America, first president of the International Geological Congress and president of the American Association for the Advancement of Science.

A dormitory at RPI was named in honor of him. It is known as Hall Hall.

It's no wonder many called him "the father of modern geology."

HARMANUS BLEECKER (1779-1849)

AMBASSADOR TO THE NETHERLANDS, CIVIC BENEFACTOR

Harmanus Bleecker was a great-great grandson of one of the original Dutch colonists who helped settle the 17th-century community of Beverwyck, the forerunner of Albany. He became a successful attorney who left a bequest of $80,000 (equal to more than $2 million today) to the city.

His legacy can be found in the Harmanus Bleecker Library (now an office building), Bleecker Stadium, Bleecker Park and Bleecker Place, off Eagle Street in the Mansion neighborhood.

He was an ambitious and brilliant young man who joined a law firm at 17, passed the bar exam and opened a law practice by the time he turned 21. He became a successful attorney and ran a training school for law students. He was a trustee of Albany Academy and the Albany Bible Society. Bleecker enjoyed teaching and took a deep interest in education. He was appointed to the board of the State Normal School (now the University at Albany) and was named a regent of the State University of New York.

He was also drawn to politics and was elected as a Federalist congressman in 1811, but grew disillusioned with Washington and returned to Albany, where he won election as a state assemblyman and served for two years. In the 1820s, his legal expertise was tapped and he was named one of New York state's commissioners who negotiated with their counterparts of New Jersey to determine a legally binding boundary between the two states.

He also was a member of

Harmanus Bleecker was a member of Congress and an ambassador to the Netherlands. He left $80,000 to the city of Albany. His grave overlooks the gorge in Section 3.

HARMANUS BLEECKER: (1779-1849)

Harmanus Bleecker's name was familiar to generations who enjoyed the library, football field and park that bore it.

the original Board of Governors that founded City Hospital, which became Albany Medical Center.

Bleecker, who was single, devoted himself to his political, humanitarian and legal work. Given his understanding of Dutch culture and his fluency in the language, he was appointed ambassador to the Netherlands in 1837 by President Martin Van Buren, a political friend from Albany. He served in the post for five years. He undertook a grand tour of Europe in 1838 at age 59 and was greeted warmly in the Netherlands, where he stayed for extended periods. Bleecker's role was largely social and administrative, and he dealt with passport matters and hosted receptions for visiting Americans in Amsterdam. He was called upon to intervene in a fight between two U.S. sailors in Rotterdam that ended up in a fatality.

His ambassadorship had one other notable consequence. He met and wed a Dutch woman 34 years his junior, Cornelia Mentz. He was 62 and she was 28 when they wed in 1841.

A year after his marriage, he stepped down as ambassador in 1842 and retired from public life and business

pursuits. He practiced law on a part-time basis and he and his wife settled in Albany. When Bleecker died in 1849, his will gave his entire estate to his widow, but it stipulated that upon her death the remainder should be used to benefit the city he loved.

His wife married Henrich Coster, a Dutch resident, and

the couple returned to Holland. When she died, an estimated $80,000 of her first husband's estate remained and it went to Albany, where generations enjoyed the public library, football and baseball fields and park that bears his name. Harmanus Bleecker was buried in a family plot, Section 3, Lot 61.

JOEL MUNSELL
(1808-1880)

PRINTER, PUBLISHER AND NOTED ALBANY CHRONICLER

oel Munsell began as a wheelwright's apprentice, learned the printing trade and with inky hands hoisted himself up the working-class ranks to become a highly respected and prosperous publisher of newspapers and books. He was welcomed into the city's cultural elite and high society as a noted antiquarian.

Some of the millions of words Munsell set in type are in private collections around the country, and his correspondence and rare books he owned are found in several archives, including the Albany Institute of History & Art, the University of Michigan and Syracuse University.

But perhaps his most lasting accomplishment, at least for historians and anyone who loves local history, was an extraordinary 10-volume collection, "Annals of Albany," an annual omnibus of news events and the quotidian rhythms of the city that he gathered between hardcovers and published between 1849 and 1859.

Munsell was born in Northfield, Mass., and attended public schools there. His father taught him the wheelwright's trade before he became a printer's apprentice in Greenfield, Mass. He proved such a bright and capable teenager that he was soon running the print shop. He moved to Albany at 19 and worked as a clerk in a downtown bookstore owned by John Denio, who quickly promoted the young man to

Joel Munsell was a respected and prosperous publisher of newspapers and books. His grave is in Section 4, Lot 47, just up the hill from the cemetery's office on South Ridge Road.

JOEL MUNSELL: (1808 - 1880)

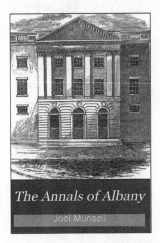

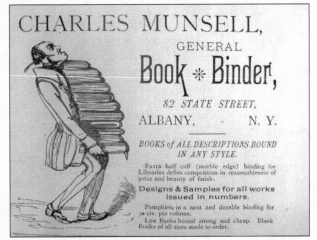

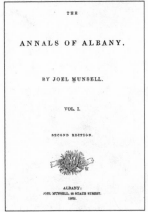

Left, cover and title page from Munsell's "The Annals of Albany." Above, an advertisement for Charles Munsell, General Book Binder in The Albany Handbook.

manager. He moonlighted as a printer and also published a small journal, the Albany Minerva, starting at age 20. He expanded his printing business and published a half-dozen small papers before the Civil War, including The Northern Star, The Freeman's Advocate, Odd Fellows' Journal and the Albany Daily Statesman.

His true passion was the history of printing and typographic art, and he researched, edited and annotated well-regarded

reference works on the craft. He was one of the founders of the Albany Institute of History & Art and for many years published the art and cultural organization's newsletter.

Munsell was revered by antiquarians, and honorary memberships in 16 historical societies from Maine to Wisconsin were conferred upon him. He outlived his first wife, Jane C. Bigelow, whom he married in 1834. He married a second time, in 1856, to Mary Reid of Montreal. His son, Frank Munsell, born in 1857, succeeded him in the printing and publishing business.

After his death, the citizens of Albany paid for a bronze tablet that was placed where he had started out as a fledgling printer, Old Gable

Hall, 58 State St. But the building was sold in 1899 and later demolished to make way for the National Commercial Bank. The tablet was removed and lost.

A daughter, Emma Munsell Hevenor, tried to reclaim her father's faded and forgotten glory. She discovered that the lost bronze tablet said that Munsell "did more than any other man to preserve the ancient records of his adopted city."

In a nice bit of historical symmetry, a descendant of Joel Munsell, Allison Munsell, works at the Albany Institute of History & Art as a digitization specialist and rights and reproduction coordinator.

Joel Munsell was buried in a family plot, Section 4, Lot 47, just up the hill from the cemetery's office on South Ridge Road. A squat gray granite obelisk lists a few of the great chronicler's accomplishments, deeply carved in clean and classical typography.

CATHARINE "KATE" HAMILTON (1781-1847)

FIRST PRIVATE BURIAL VAULT IN CEMETERY

atharine "Kate" Hamilton and the uncertainty surrounding the fate of her private burial vault, the first of its kind in the cemetery, is an enduring Albany Rural mystery.

She was the wife of Isaac Hamilton, a lawyer and Albany alderman, and they lived at a fashionable downtown address, 353 Lydius St., which no longer exists. It was in the South End near the Pastures neighborhood.

Hamilton was widowed in 1834 when her husband died at age 55, leaving her to raise their son. Her husband was eulogized as a public servant who "evinced a noble disinterestedness of character, and elevated views of public duty and public virtue."

She outlived him by 13 years. Her funeral procession left the Baptist Church on North Pearl Street on the afternoon of Feb. 6, 1847, and included a long line of horse-drawn carriages. She was placed in a private vault, the first such burial in the three years since Albany Rural was formally consecrated in 1844. The vault was located in Section 5, Lot 23, near the foot of South Ridge Road, just up from the cemetery office.

Hamilton had very specific wishes about her funeral rites. In her will, she wrote that after her remains were locked in the vine-covered vault, the "lock should be filled with lead and the keys thrown into the Hudson River." Accounts of the service indicated that this was done.

Rumors circulated that a large amount of cash was

Catharine Hamilton's vine-covered tomb, circa 1940. An 1871 guide noted it would likely fall or be taken down due to poor construction.

buried with her, and initial break-in attempts were unsuccessful. But in 1868, more determined grave robbers blew off the lock and broke through a brick wall. But they were unable to breach Hamilton's stone coffin. In addition to the damage caused by the thwarted burglars, the vault was showing signs of structural failure due to shoddy construction.

It is unclear when Hamilton's vault was removed, but all that remains today is a plain stone marker.

All that remains of Catharine Hamilton's burial vault in Section 5 just up from the cemetery office.

ROBERT YATES (1738-1801)

LEADING PATRIOT, DELEGATE TO THE FIRST U.S. CONSTITUTIONAL CONVENTION, ANTI-FEDERALIST

Robert Yates was a leading figure during the American Revolution and a delegate to the first U.S. Constitutional Convention who remained loyal to his anti-Federalist sympathies, which opposed creation of a stronger, centralized federal government.

Yates was an independent-minded contrarian who withdrew from the Constitutional Convention in 1787 in Philadelphia because he believed the committee had overstepped its powers. He refused to yield to political pressure, stood his ground and authored an infamous anti-Federalist paper, No. 84, under a non de plume, that proposed the Constitution should not be adopted unless it contained a Bill of Rights.

Yates was born and raised in Schenectady's Stockade. His father, Joseph Yates, was the first mayor of Schenectady and was later elected state senator and governor.

Robert studied law in New York City and was admitted to the New York Bar in 1760. He moved to Albany and became an alderman and was a supporter of the Radical Whigs, a political party dedicated to protecting liberty. His legal background was

At top, a detail and above the full headstone of Robert Yates.

called upon in the drafting of a 1775 resolution opposing the "several arbitrary and oppressive acts of the British Parliament" that led to the colonists' demands for independence.

Yates was selected to represent Albany County in four provincial Congresses, and he arranged for a newly copied Declaration of Independence to be carried to Albany on July 14, 1776. Under Yates' order, the document was published in Albany newspapers and read in its entirety July 19 on the front steps of City Hall.

He ran unsuccessfully for governor in 1789. Yates later served as a judge of the state Supreme Court and was chief judge from 1790 to 1798. Critics accused him of being overly lenient to Loyalists. Although Federalist leaders Alexander Hamilton and James Madison are remembered by historians for spearheading the effort to adopt and ratify the Constitution, Yates, an important anti-Federalist responsible for championing the notion of a Bill of Rights, is largely unknown today.

Yates died Sept. 9, 1801. He was buried in a family plot, marked by a simple gray sandstone obelisk in Section 8, Lot 1, a third of the way up South Ridge Road, on the edge of the Moordanaers Kill ravine.

The plot had become severely overgrown and neglected and trees felled by storms knocked over some of the markers. In recent years, descendants of the Yates family volunteered and led work parties to clear brush and cut down trees in an effort to restore some of the faded glory of a long-forgotten patriot who was a central figure in America's struggle for independence.

ARCHIBALD MCINTYRE
(1772-1858)

STATE COMPTROLLER, OWNED LARGE IRON ORE MINE IN ADIRONDACKS

Archibald McIntyre was a Scottish immigrant whose ambition and industry propelled him to leading ranks in politics and business. He was a state legislator, state comptroller and the architect of the state's first lotteries. In business, he developed large and prosperous iron ore mines in the Adirondacks, and a mountain range in the High Peaks was named for him.

He is the patriarch of a prominent family, its history darkened by a famous Adirondack tragedy. The McIntyre plot is located in a shaded, remote section a short distance up South Ridge Road, Section 9, Lot 5, along a ravine overlooking the Moordanaers Kill. McIntyre was a founder and original trustee of Albany Rural Cemetery, which gave him an early choice for his plot.

An old, tumbledown cast-iron fence and a spectacular sarcophagus carved to look like a funereal urn dedicated to the patriarch dominates the plot. It was designed by noted sculptor Robert E. Launitz. Thistles carved into grave markers are symbols of Scotland, and the range of family members buried there reinforces the clannish nature of the Scots.

The marble monuments are streaked with lichen and mold, which adds to a melancholy mood that permeates the circular plot.

McIntyre was a founder and the first secretary of the St. Andrew's Society. The Scottish fraternal organization was founded in 1803

State Comptroller Archibald McIntyre ran an iron ore mine in Tahawus near Mount Marcy in the Adirondacks. The McIntyre family grave is located in Section 9 of the cemetery.

ARCHIBALD MCINTYRE: (1772 - 1858)

for social and benevolent purposes. It also provided charitable relief for newly arrived Scottish immigrants and others. The society purchased two large plots in the cemetery for the burials of Scottish immigrants who had no family in the area or were too poor to afford their own plot. The society's elegant brownstone at 150 Washington Ave. in Albany still hosts social events and is known as "The Rooms."

McIntyre was born in Kenmore, Scotland, and emigrated with his family to America when he was 2 years old. They settled in New York City. He married Elizabeth McDonald, and the couple had seven children. They moved to a farm in Montgomery County. McIntyre was first elected as a state assemblyman from his rural district at age 19. He was re-elected for seven terms and was appointed state comptroller in 1806. He served in that capacity for the next 15 years and became a trusted adviser to Gov. DeWitt Clinton during his drive to build the Erie Canal. As comptroller, McIntyre also developed the state's first lotteries, or games of chance. He moved with his family to Albany in 1834.

McIntyre and his brother-in-law, Malcolm McMartin, founded the Elba Iron and Steel Manufacturing Co. in North Elba, Essex County, in the mid-1830s. They expected to find silver veins in the Adirondacks, but instead found rich deposits of iron ore. They built the first blast furnace in 1838 and began

Gravestones for Dr. James McNaughton, left, and David Henderson, above, are in the McIntyre family plot.

acquiring large tracts of forest lands that they clear-cut to fuel the massive furnaces that generated the extreme heat needed to smelt out iron from the ore. They situated the Upper Works in the town of Newcomb, along the torrents of the upper Hudson River, which powered the furnace's bellows. McIntyre's iron mining operation built a company town of employee cabins at Tahawus, also called McIntyre, near Mount Marcy.

It was here, on Sept. 14, 1901, that Vice-President Theodore Roosevelt, after climbing Mount Marcy, learned that President William McKinley had been shot in Buffalo. Roosevelt was later sworn in as the 26th president, at 42 the youngest in the nation's history.

The McIntyre plot in Albany Rural includes the graves of his sons-in-law, Dr. James McNaughton, a president of Albany Medical College, and David Henderson, who was a director of the mining company and an innovator in

mining techniques.

On Sept. 3, 1845, Henderson, his 10-year-old son and guide John Cheney were on a hike looking for ways to increase water flow for the iron mines when a rifle in his backpack accidentally discharged and killed Henderson. He was 52.

The pond where he died was renamed Calamity Pond; the stream that flows through it was called Calamity Brook. There is a large memorial marker at the site, the only one of its kind allowed in the Adirondack wilderness. Hikers heading to Mount Marcy from the Tahawus side pass the marker that recalls the tragedy.

McIntyre outlived his son-in-law by 13 years and died in 1858. The McIntyre mountain range in the Adirondacks, also spelled MacIntyre, is named for the patriarch.

EDWARD CORNELIUS DELAVAN (1793-1871)

HOTEL OWNER, WINE IMPORTER, TEMPERANCE MOVEMENT LEADER

E dward Corne-
lius Delavan
was the owner
of the famous
downtown
hotel and restaurant the
Delavan House, notorious for
open bribery and assorted
shenanigans of state legislators during the Tammany
Hall era. The booze flowed
freely at his hotel, and he was
a successful wine merchant
who, later in life, did an
about-face and became a
rabid teetotaler and fanatical
leader of a national temperance movement.

Delavan was born and
raised in Westchester
County, and his father died
when he was 8. He moved to
Albany with his mother, two
sisters and a brother. Edward
became an apprentice in
a printer's office at 13. He
left to work at his brother's
Albany hardware store.

The brothers began visit-
ing Europe in 1814 to find
more wine sources for their
burgeoning wine import-
ing business. Delavan also
branched out and began
speculating on real estate.
He shrewdly bought parcels

around the Erie Canal before
it was being developed and
the land rose sharply in
value. He made considerable
profit and in 1829 helped
found the Canal Bank of
Albany.

That same year, he was
recruited by the Rev. Na-
thaniel Hewitt and became
an anti-alcohol proselytizer
and extremist. Convinced of
the evils of liquor, he began
spending large sums to back
the temperance movement
and formed the New York
State Temperance Society.
He reportedly dumped all

Edward C. Delavan was a wealthy wine merchant and proprietor of the Delavan House, Albany's grandest hotel at the time. His burial monument is in Section 53 along side Middle Ridge Road.

EDWARD CORNELIUS DELAVAN: (1793 - 1871)

Images show the Delavan House in Albany, undated.

the bottles of his valuable wine cellar into the street.

He was joined in temperance activities by his friend Dr. Eliphalet Nott, a Presbyterian minister who became president of Union College. Delavan became a longtime college trustee and a major donor. He gave Union a notable collection of minerals and shells in 1858.

Delavan bankrolled temperance newspapers and became a national leader of the cause. He was elected chairman of the American Temperance Union in 1836. He argued against the use of sacramental wine in church services, controversial even among temperance supporters. He traveled to Italy and France and railed against the wine culture from which he had once profited.

In 1844, Delavan built his eponymous hotel, widely regarded as the finest hotel and restaurant in the city, a six-story structure on Broadway across from Union Station at present-day Tricentennial Park. Luminaries and political hacks gathered there, along with ladies of the night. According to numerous accounts, it was not a dry establishment, although Delavan never publicly discussed that apparent contradiction.

During the Civil War, he sent a million copies of a temperance tract to soldiers in the Union Army.

Delavan was married twice, first to Abby Smith, who died in 1848, and a second time in 1850 to Harriet Ann Schuyler. The couple had one child and

they settled in Ballston Spa. In 1860, Delavan's net worth was estimated at $625,000, about $16 million in today's dollars.

Liquor-free towns in Wisconsin and Illinois were named in his honor.

Delavan was buried in a family plot, Section 53, Lot 10, halfway up Middle Ridge Road, with a large marble monument topped

with a cross.

Although Delavan had been dead for 25 years at the time, the Delavan House is remembered most for a Dec. 30, 1894, fire that killed 19 people. It was one of the city's deadliest fires and many of the victims were young chambermaids. The fire was fictionalized in William Kennedy's 1996 novel, "The Flaming Corsage."

Dyer Lathrop
(1787-1855)

Albany Orphan Asylum Founder, Father-in-Law of Rail Baron Leland Stanford

Dyer Lathrop was a man of significant accomplishments, an Albany merchant and philanthropist who helped found the Albany Orphan Asylum. But his daughter's marriage to railroad tycoon Leland Stanford was the reason he ended up with the largest monument in all of Albany Rural Cemetery, a granite obelisk that is astonishing both for its sheer mass and its exquisite artistry.

The elegantly carved monument soars more than 30 feet, a solid block of stone weighing untold tons, topped by a large-scale sculpture of a Greek goddess in a mourning pose. It was the gift of his daughter, Jane Lathrop Stanford, and her husband, Leland, who co-founded Stanford University.

Dyer Lathrop was born in New London, Conn., and moved to Albany, where he set up a downtown wholesale and retail shop that sold a variety of goods. He married Jane Anne Shields of Albany,

in 1824. He was 37 and she was 21. Her father, Daniel Shields, was a Revolutionary War soldier and ended up as a state employee, serving as the sergeant-at-arms for the state Assembly.

The couple had seven children, although one died in infancy. After several years of home-schooling, they sent their second-oldest child, Jane Elizabeth, born in 1828, to the Albany Female Academy (Albany Academy for Girls today), one of the first schools for girls in the

The monument to merchant and philanthropist Dyer Lathrop is the largest in Albany Rural Cemetery. The more-than-30-foot granite obelisk honors the first treasurer of the Albany Orphan Asylum.

DYER LATHROP: (1787-1855)

country. Nicknamed Jennie, she was a good student and graduated in 1845 from the private all-girls' school, where daughters of the city's elite were educated.

At the same time, at his downtown store, Lathrop encountered poor, unfortunate street urchins who had been left orphaned and begged for food and money from merchants and their customers. Their grim existence moved the father of six to try to help these neglected youths.

Lathrop met Orissa Healy and Eliza Wilcox, good-hearted and civic-minded women who had a dream of founding the Albany Orphan Asylum. It was Healy's idea following the death of her baby in childbirth, abandonment by her husband and a resulting depression. In 1829, she and Wilcox took the first steps to assist orphans and to provide them a home. She turned to the city's merchants and men of means in Albany to make it a reality.

Dyer Lathrop was one who responded to her appeal for financial support and organizational help. Lathrop was elected treasurer in 1830 on the first board of directors, serving with his friend, Edward C. Delevan, the hotelier and restaurateur, who agreed to become the first president of the Albany Orphan Asylum.

Meanwhile, in 1850, Lathrop's 22-year-old daughter Jane married a young lawyer, Leland Stanford of Watervliet, and the newlyweds settled in Port Washington, Wis., where her husband had a law

The Dyer Lathrop monument, overlooking the Moordanaers Kill, is topped with a Greek goddess in a mourning pose.

practice. His office and law library were destroyed by fire in 1852 and, despondent, he left to join his five brothers in California. The Stanford brothers sold goods and supplies to prospectors chasing the riches of the gold rush.

Jane felt unhappy and abandoned in Wisconsin, where she had few friends, and at her family's urging she returned in 1852 to live at her parents' home in Albany. She spent the next three years caring for her ill father, but she was sad over being separated from her husband. She also had to endure the gossip of Albany society, who whispered that the long-distance marriage had foundered and was in trouble.

Dyer Lathrop died April 18, 1855, and Jane convinced her

husband to return to Albany. After the funeral, she happily relocated to her husband's modest house in Sacramento, Calif., and the couple eventually brought Jane's mother, sister and three brothers to live with them out West.

In 1861, a watershed year for the Stanfords, Leland became president of the Central Pacific Railroad and governor of California. They moved to a mansion in the state's capital and used some of their newfound wealth to erect the extraordinary monument to Jane's father, Dyer Lathrop, which dominates the family plot, Section 11, Lot 21, halfway up South Ridge Road along a wooded perimeter near the edge of the ravine overlooking the Moordanaers Kill.

LEARNED HAND
(1872-1961)

Learned Hand was a federal appeals court judge, a superb craftsman of the law and an erudite philosopher widely considered to be one of the greatest judges ever. He was spoken of in the same breath as Oliver Wendell Holmes, Louis Brandeis and Benjamin Cardozo. Although he was never named to the nation's highest court, he was nicknamed the "10th man on the U.S. Supreme Court" because of his towering intellect and sterling reputation. He was the most-quoted judge among legal scholars, the subject of an 818-page biography published in 1994.

His unusual name was chosen by his parents, Samuel and Lydia Hand. He was named after his mother's father, Billings Learned, and was christened Billings Learned Hand. He grew up on fashionable lower State Street in downtown Albany. Law was the family business. His father, two uncles and grandfather were prominent lawyers and judges in Albany. His father was a close political adviser to Gov. Samuel Tilden and the Albany Regency, but turned down offers of a state Supreme Court judgeship to run as governor to succeed Tilden. He did agree to serve briefly on the state's highest court, the New York Court of Appeals.

His father's death when he was 14 wounded Hand deeply, and he tried hard to measure up. He graduated near the top of his class at Albany Academy and entered Harvard University in 1889. Although he said he was unhappy and felt socially awkward, he was elected president of the Harvard Advocate and graduated summa

Learned Hand, U.S. judge and judicial philosopher, is buried in a family plot in Section 11, Lot 14, off South Ridge Road overlooking the Moordanaers Kill ravine with his wife, Frances Fincke.

LEARNED HAND: (1872-1961)

cum laude while earning both a bachelor's and master's degree in four years. He began Harvard Law School, without pause, in 1893.

After graduating, he returned to Albany and joined the law firm of Marcus T. Hun. His briefs sparkled, and other firms tried to hire him to write theirs. But Hand longed to argue cases in court and he took on pro bono work for courtroom experience. At night, he taught classes at Albany Law School. During a violent 1901 trolley car strike against United Traction Co., workers who crossed the picket line were injured in rock-throwing attacks, igniting riots. The National Guard was called in to restore order and outnumbered soldiers opened fire on the unruly mob and killed two people.

Hand was appointed by the state to investigate charges of brutality on the part of police and National Guard soldiers. He completed a thorough investigation and cleared the officers, but he was critical of the soldiers.

In 1902, Hand, a 30-year-old bachelor who had little experience dating, married Frances Fincke. They moved to New York City and Hand went to work for a Wall Street firm. The couple had three daughters.

He became active in politics and joined the movement to reform corrupt Tammany Hall. In 1909, Hand was recommended for a federal judgeship in Manhattan. He worked long hours and wrote opinions on important issues of the times, including a com-

The plain gray granite marker marks the grave of the man said to be one of the greatest judges ever.

plex obscenity case and the protection given to political dissenters who criticize government leaders under the First Amendment's freedom of speech.

During his relentless hours at the office and long absences, his wife took up with Louis Dow, a professor of French at Dartmouth College. Their unusually intimate relationship pained Hand, but it continued for 30 years, until Dow's death in 1944.

Hand practiced as much patience, fortitude and self-restraint in his personal life as he did in his work as a judge. Although he dealt with thousands of cases and served longer than any federal judge in history, his careful consideration of the facts and his brilliant writing did not tilt toward either a liberal or a conservative agenda. He was famous for 4-mile walks around Manhattan and singing off-color sea songs during his daily constitutionals, while taking a break from his work on the

Court of Appeals.

Perhaps his most famous case came about because the U.S. Supreme Court was unable to muster a quorum to hear United States v. Aluminum Co. of America. Congress enacted a special statute designating the Court of Appeals for the Second District as the court of last resort to hear the case. Hand wrote the landmark opinion in 1944 that established key principles of anti-trust law.

He later published "The Spirit of Liberty," a popular collection of essays and explanation of the Constitution of the United States. He was a founding member of the American Law Institute. He served on the Second Circuit court until June 1961 and died two months later of a heart attack. His wife died two years later. Both are buried in a family plot, Section 11, Lot 14, off South Ridge Road overlooking the Moordanaers Kill ravine. The couple's names are carved side by side on the front of a plain gray granite marker.

JOHN ALDEN DIX
(1860-1928)

NEW YORK GOVERNOR, FAMOUS UNDERACHIEVER

J ohn Alden Dix served as New York's 38th governor from 1911 to 1912, achieved little in office and fell into political obscurity. Perhaps he is best known as an underachiever and a college dropout. He is often mistakenly given credit as the namesake of Dix Mountain and the Dix Range in the High Peaks of the Adirondack Mountains. He was not that Dix.

That Dix was John Adams Dix (1798-1872), who was governor, a U.S. senator, U.S. Secretary of the Treasury and a Union Army general during the Civil War. Newspaper reporters often referred to John Alden Dix as his nephew or a first cousin once removed. They were not related.

John Alden Dix was born in Glens Falls on Christmas Day, 1860. He was one of four children of marble quarry owner James Lawton Dix and his wife, Laura Stevens Dix. John graduated from Glens Falls Academy and attended Cornell University for three years but did not graduate. He went to work in his father's quarry and also in another family business, a Glens Falls machine shop.

Dix's father helped set him up in a lumber business outside Schuylerville, and Dix married his partner's daughter, Gertrude Thom-

The burial site of John Alden Dix, who was New York's 38th governor, and that of his wife and her parents.

son. Dix made a fortune in lumber and diversified by founding the Iroquois Pulp & Paper Co. He acquired 17,000 acres of timberland in Herkimer County, which supplied his mills.

Dix moved into politics, starting as chairman of the Washington County Democratic Committee. In 1908, Dix was the Democratic nominee for lieutenant governor on the ticket with Lewis Stuyvesant Chanler, who was trounced by Republican Charles Evan Hughes.

In the gubernatorial election of 1910, with the Republicans divided between the Old Guard who backed William Howard Taft and reformers who supported Theodore Roosevelt, Dix defeated GOP candidate Henry L. Stimson by a thin margin.

Dix was the first Democratic governor elected in New York in 16 years, and the Democratic sweep included a majority in both the state Assembly and Senate.

As governor, Tammany Hall-backed Dix could not extricate himself from the internal battles of the Tammany forces, and his progressive legislation proposals got lost in the fray. Dix was considered an indecisive and ineffective governor. The New York Times sniped: "It begins to look as if there was nobody in the State quite so careless about the success and the reputation of Gov. Dix's administration as the Governor himself."

On Dix's watch, the Triangle Shirtwaist Co. in New York City caught fire on March 25, 1911, and killed

JOHN ALDEN DIX: (1860-1928)

146 workers. The vast majority were women and girls, the youngest just 14. An investigation determined that some doorways were locked and all were killed in the conflagration within 18 minutes after it began. Dix established a New York State Factory Commission to investigate factory conditions and 32 worker safety bills became state laws as a result.

On March 29, 1911, four days after the Triangle Shirtwaist fire, fire broke out in the state Capitol. A night watchman, Samuel Abbott, was killed and the fire destroyed nearly the entire State Library, including 500,000 books and 300,000 manuscripts, and caused severe damage to the historic building. In the wake of the two fires, state legislation was passed that enhanced fire safety regulations and strengthened building codes.

Dix was credited with a few accomplishments as governor. He created the State Conservation Commission, signed a law authorizing direct primary elections and improved state highways. He also helped pass the 54-hour workweek that required one day of rest in seven. It set limits for the first time on the number of working hours for women and children in factories.

At the state Democratic convention in Syracuse in 1912, Dix lost the party's nomination to William Sulzer. Nine months after he was sworn in, Sulzer became New York's first and only governor to be impeached.

Grave marker of John Alden Dix and his wife, Gertude Thomson.

Detail of Dix's headstone.

Weary of state politics, Dix and his wife moved in 1913 to Santa Barbara, Calif., and retreated to private life. Gertrude Dix died at 63 on Dec. 18, 1923, in Santa Barbara. The former governor died in New York City of heart disease on April 9, 1928. He was 67. The couple had no children.

Dix and his wife were interred in Section 41, Lot 11. Their gray granite marker is intricately carved with lilies, a cross and symbols for alpha and omega, Greek

The headstone of John Alden Dix's parents-in-law, Lemon and Abby Thomson.

letters, that reference Jesus Christ and eternity. The plot was purchased by his wife's parents, Lemon and Abby Thomson, and they are also buried there.

James Bentley "Cy" Seymour (1878-1919)

National League batting champion

SEYMOUR, N.Y. Nat'L

J ames Bentley "Cy" Seymour was one of the greatest hitters in the history of Major League Baseball and a fine pitcher, too, but he is largely lost to history by all but the most devoted aficionados of the sport. It was said of Seymour that "only Babe Ruth was more versatile."

And yet Seymour's final resting place is unmarked. He is buried next to a small gravestone for his wife, Agnes Seymour, in a nondescript plot in Section 15, Lot 46, that was purchased by his parents.

His burial anonymity belies turn-of-the-century stardom, when Seymour filled baseball stadiums and won the 1905 National League batting crown with a .377 average. He also led the league in hits, doubles and RBIs and fell one short of the most home runs.

Seymour, who was born in Albany, started out as a pitcher. His blinding fastball earned him the nickname "the Cyclone," or "Cy" for short. He pitched for the New York Giants from 1896 to 1900 and led the league in strikeouts in 1898, winning a career-best 25 games that year, the sixth-most wins in all of baseball. But the 6-foot, 200-pound lefty was wild and struggled to control his fastball. His career as a

pitcher ended in 1900, when he suffered the dreaded "dead arm" injury.

Seymour reinvented himself as a center fielder known for his clutch hitting, and he jumped to the Baltimore Orioles of the upstart American League in 1901. The next year, he signed with the Reds

and steadily improved his batting average until 1905, when he pulled off what was called "one of the most remarkable hitting performances in Reds history."

Even with his skills declining, the Reds sold Seymour to the Giants in 1906 for an eye-popping $10,000, the biggest price paid for a player at that point. He didn't know when to hang up his spikes and played into his 40s on minor-league teams. He worked in a New York City shipyard during World I, contracted tuberculosis and died of the disease Sept. 20, 1919. He was 46.

Seymour had 1,724 hits,

The unmarked grave of James Bentley Seymour and the grave marker of his wife, Agnes Seymour. Above, Seymour's 1909 baseball card.

a lifetime batting average of .303 and a 61-56 record as a pitcher. Babe Ruth was the only player with more hits and more wins as a pitcher.

But the Reds' all-time leader in both single-season and career batting was not offered membership into the Reds Hall of Fame until 1998, nearly a century after he played his last game for the team and 40 years after the Reds Hall of Fame was established.

JACK MCAULIFFE
(1866-1937)

WORLD LIGHTWEIGHT BOXING CHAMPION

Jack McAuliffe became the lightweight boxing champion of the world in 1887 and was one of only three titleholders who retired undefeated. Some boxing experts have ranked him among the top five lightweights of all-time, while others dismiss his record because he fought during a time in the sport when there were few rules.

Known as "Napoleon of the Ring," McAuliffe was a star during the bare-knuckle era, when brutal and bloody bouts could grind on for more than 70 rounds. The 5-foot-6, 135-pounder was heralded for silky "cat-quick" movements around the ring, a wicked, twisting left jab that opened cuts on opponents and a flurry of combi-nations that often resulted in knockouts.

Born in Cork, Ireland, McAuliffe emigrated with his family at age 5 to Bangor, Maine, and started boxing there. He turned pro in 1883 and won the world lightweight title three years later.

His title bout was against English champion Jem Carney on Nov. 16, 1887, and the two pugilists pounded

The headstone of Jack McAuliffe, a world lightweight champion boxer who retired in 1893. McAuliffe lived a lavish lifestyle and was known as "the Napoleon of the Ring."

JACK McAULIFFE: (1866-1937)

each other for 78 rounds. The fight ended in a controversial draw after American fans stormed the ring when Carney knocked down McAuliffe for the third time. After the rabble was quieted, both fighters left the ring and each claimed he was world champion.

McAuliffe's biggest payday was a $5,000 title fight against Billy Dacey in 1888. McAuliffe knocked out the highly regarded challenger in 11 rounds.

McAuliffe settled in the Williamsburg neighborhood of Brooklyn and embraced his celebrity. He dated ingenues and twice married stage actresses. He enjoyed fine dining, fancy clothes, expensive cigars and was dubbed "the Dapper Dan of the ring." His lavish lifestyle often cut into his training time, and he continued to win with natural talent despite not always fighting in peak condition.

He also was an inveterate gambler and a denizen of racetracks who squandered his fortune. He retired in 1894, made a comeback in 1896, but his carousing and diminishing skills had caught up with him by then, and he took a few beatings before retiring for good after a 1897 bout against Tommy Ryan of Philadelphia. After his career in the ring, he scratched out a living as a bookmaker and an occasional vaudeville performer.

McAuliffe ended up with an official record of 31 wins (22 by knockout), six draws and no losses. He died of

complications from throat cancer at his home in Queens on Nov. 5, 1937. He was broke and had made no arrangements for his death. A stepdaughter and her husband, Sadie and James Campbell, of Lake George, paid to have his body shipped by train to the cemetery and "the Napoleon of the Ring" was buried in their plot, Section 15, Lot 73. McAuliffe was inducted into the Ring Boxing

Boxer Jack McAuliffe is displayed in this 1893 Red Cross Tobacoo boxing card, performing the cross buttock move on boxer Tommy Ryan. In 1897, McAuliffe fought Ryan in his last fight before retiring. The fight ended in a draw.

Hall of Fame in 1954 and the International Boxing Hall of Fame in Canastota, Madison County, in 1995.

JAMES FAMILY PLOT (1771-1832)

PATRIARCH WILLIAM JAMES AND RELATIVES OF NOVELIST HENRY JAMES

Patriarch William James is a quintessential American success story. He was a dirt-poor Irish farm boy who sailed to the new world with a few coins in his pocket, and through grit and good luck as a store clerk, he came to own a downtown Albany dry goods store, branched out into other businesses, speculated in real estate and amassed a huge fortune. His descendants built upon his financial success and achieved a legacy of international renown highlighted in the work of his grandsons: the pioneer of American psychology William James and his brother,

Henry James, a celebrated writer known as the father of the modern novel.

In an acclaimed and monumental 1991 family history, "The Jameses: A Family Narrative," Pulitzer Prize-winning biographer R.W.B. Lewis called the James family "perhaps the most remarkable family the country has ever known as regards its literary and intellectual accomplishments."

The James family plot is located in the central part of the cemetery halfway up South Ridge Road, Section 16, Lot 1, a brooding space shaded by ancient evergreens and encircled by a tumbledown cast-iron fence

around a cluster of crumbling brownstone monuments. It is drenched in symbolism and tinged with melancholy, not unlike a scene from a Henry James novel. A stout stone post guards the entrance, lichen-covered and carved with an inverted torch, which symbolizes death or a life extinguished, representing the passing of the soul into the next life.

Records show that the James family purchased the plot for $541.40 on July 1, 1848. The patriarch's remains were reinterred here from a downtown church burial ground, and his name is carved on the largest monument, topped with a

The James family plot includes the patriarch, businessman and land speculator William James, as well as his son, Henry James Sr., and grandson William James, a philosopher.

JAMES FAMILY PLOT: (1771-1832)

shroud-covered urn, another popular symbol of death.

William James made his home at 70 N. Pearl St., near today's Steuben Athletic Club, and the place was crawling with kids. James had 13 children by three wives. He owned a bustling dry goods store on the southwest corner of State and Green streets and grew it into a chain of stores. He also owned a salt company, a tobacco factory and a Hudson River shipping operation.

He was a catalyst in building the Erie Canal and was a major land speculator for whom "lands and houses came into his possession like filings to a magnet," according to the Albany Daily Advertiser. At one point, James held the mortgages on nearly the entire city of Syracuse and on the campus of Union College. He left an estate estimated at $3 million when he died 10 days shy of his 61st birthday in 1832, second only to John Jacob Astor's fortune in New York at the time. Downtown Albany's Middle Lane was changed to James Street after his death, and an obituary called him "prosperous almost beyond parallel ... the man who has done more to build up the city of Albany than any other individual."

The patriarch's son, Henry James Sr., was a troublemaker who stopped each day on his way to Albany Academy, starting at age 10, for a nip of raw gin or brandy at a cobbler's shop. He burned himself badly at the age of 13 in a mishap involving a turpentine-soaked balloon

The grave of William James, left, and the marker for Mary Temple, an inspiration for brother Henry James' literary works.

he had sent aloft from the school grounds and endured the pain of having his right leg amputated above the knee without benefit of anesthesia, which did not exist then. He was later fitted with a wooden leg. He dropped out of Union College his senior year and squandered a fortune on expensive cigars, oyster dinners and fancy clothes. He eventually got his diploma at Union and his inheritance of a $10,000 annuity (about $300,000 today) allowed him to travel abroad frequently. He befriended Emerson, Thoreau, Thackeray, Carlyle and other luminaries. George Bernard Shaw called him "the most interesting member of his family." A homegrown philosopher influenced by the theology of Emanuel Swedenborg, he developed the concept of "spiritual creationism."

He is buried in the family plot as is his son, William James, the patriarch's grandson, a philosopher who coined the term "stream of

consciousness" and wrote the seminal two-volume work, "The Principles of Psychology." He was the architect of a philosophy known as pragmatism.

His brother, Henry James, is not buried here. But he did come to the family plot to attend a funeral for Mary Temple in March 1870. Records show the great writer paid for her burial and monument. Temple was orphaned by her parents' death in 1854, and James was enamored of her beauty and personality. She is the source material of his greatest fictional female characters, including Daisy Miller in the eponymous novella, and Isabel Archer in "The Portrait of a Lady," which is set partly in Albany.

On the brownstone monument for Mary Temple, Henry James directed the stone carvers to chisel out a small star beside her name. It signifies that she was beloved by the famous novelist and was his little star. It is the only symbol of the sort in that position among tens of thousands of carved stone markers and monuments in the cemetery.

MARCUS T. REYNOLDS (1869-1937)

Marcus T. Reynolds is widely considered to be the greatest architect that Albany ever produced. His sublime interpretations of the Dutch Revival style at once honored the historic city's Dutch past while they transformed and elevated a mundane and decaying downtown cityscape.

He designed three dozen buildings around the city, many of them with a Dutch flavor, including the Albany Trust Co., First National Bank of Albany, Albany City Savings Bank, United Traction Co. Build-ing, Albany Academy and Hackett Middle School and the Gideon Putnam Hotel in Saratoga Springs. Several of his buildings are listed on the National Register of Historic Places.

The D&H Building on Broadway at the foot of State Street is regarded as Reynolds' masterpiece. It was inspired by the Cloth Hall at Ypres, Belgium. Constructed as the headquarters of the Delaware & Hudson Railway Co., it features ornate towers, dormers, filigree and Flemish Gothic flourishes clad in gray cast stone. It was completed in 1918, after six years of construction, at a cost of $1.25 million.

It is now the headquarters of the State University of New York's central administration.

Some scholars prefer Reynolds' smaller gems, such as Truck House No. 4, a fire station at the corner of Delaware Avenue and Marshall Street, that is a loving homage to Dutch Revivalism. It reflects Reynolds' richly detailed style that makes use of decorative elements such as pediments, pilasters, cartouches, swags and finials.

Banks were a specialty of his Albany architectural firm, and he designed bank buildings in Hudson, Catskill

The grave of prominent Albany architect Marcus T. Reynolds. Reynolds designed a variety of banks as well as Albany landmarks and notable Albany Rural Cemetery monuments.

MARCUS T. REYNOLDS: (1869 - 1937)

and Amsterdam, as well as the Cooperstown railroad station and other buildings in Schenectady and Saratoga Springs.

Reynolds' architectural artistry can also be seen at Albany Rural Cemetery, where he designed several prominent monuments and major elements on the grounds, including the classical Broadway gate, the superintendent's house and a caretaker's cottage at the south gate. He also served as a board member of the cemetery.

Reynolds was born in Great Barrington, Mass., but he lived most of his life at 98 Columbia St. in downtown Albany. He attended Albany Academy (at its original location across from City Hall, not the school he later designed) and graduated from St. Paul's School in Concord, N.H., in 1886. He graduated in 1890 from Williams College, where he was an avid photographer who documented architectural details of the campus. He earned a master's degree in architecture from Columbia University in 1893 and wrote a thesis titled "Housing of the Poor in American Cities" that scholars still reference. He traveled across Europe for the next two years and studied Renaissance architecture.

Reynolds came from old Dutch stock. His family was related by marriage to the Van Rensselaers and his paternal grandfather, also Marcus Tullius Reynolds, was a prominent Albany attorney, a Congressman, state

The Delaware & Hudson Building is considered Reynolds' masterpiece.

Supreme Court justice and president of three railroad lines, including the Albany & Northern (whose tracks still intersect Cemetery Avenue at the Broadway entrance to the cemetery). His father, Dexter Reynolds, a close friend and classmate of future President Chester A. Arthur at Union College, graduated from Harvard Law School in 1850, practiced law in Albany and wrote a book on insurance law. He served as a Union Army officer during the Civil War and was a land speculator who bought more than 200,000 acres in Iowa. He also was a prolific inventor with more than 20 patents, including an automatic positioning of printers' type that was so efficient it was fought by the Printers Guild because it took away printers' jobs. His mother was Catherine Cuyler Reynolds, a leading figure of Albany society.

Reynolds' great-nephew, Stephen Reynolds, 80, a retired attorney, recounted

boyhood memories in a Times Union interview in June 2013 for a story marking the 100th anniversary of the D&H Building. "Marcus was the family patriarch and the stories were passed down to us as kids, which we had to learn by heart," he said. He said the great architect was a lifelong bachelor who entertained many lady friends, lived in luxury, traveled often to Europe and displayed eccentricities. He donned a white glove before shaking the hand of a worker at a building site and said, "I don't know where that hand has been."

Marcus' brother, Cuyler Reynolds, was a notable Albany historian and writer. He published the multi-volume history, "Albany Chronicles" and several important genealogical texts. He was the city historian, the first curator of the Albany Institute of History & Art and its director for 10 years. He acquired more than 1,000 books on local history in the institute's collection.

The extensive archives of drawings and other architectural material of his famous brother were given to the institute.

Marcus T. Reynolds, the architect, his brother Cuyler, his father, mother, grandfather and other family members are buried in a circular family plot, Section 17, Lot 1, midway up South Ridge Road, dominated by a graceful brownstone obelisk with classical details that would not look out of place on a Reynolds design.

PHOEBE HARRIS PHELPS (1818-1889)

DOMESTIC VIOLENCE SURVIVOR

Phoebe Harris Phelps was a victim of domestic abuse, a survivor of monstrous maltreatment and a mother of three who overcame horrific circumstances to publish books on religious themes.

She was rescued, harbored and befriended by Susan B. Anthony, the suffragist and champion of women's rights.

Born into a prominent family, Phoebe graduated in 1835 from the Albany Female Academy (now Al-

bany Academy for Girls) and taught there for a few years. She married Charles Abner Phelps, an 1841 Union College graduate who completed Harvard Medical School and went into practice in Boston with his father. She raised their three daughters as he pursued his political ambitions. He was elected to the Massachusetts state legislature in 1855 and eventually rose to the position of speaker.

The abuse began in 1858, according to Phoebe's writ-

ten accounts. When she caught him with a mistress at their Beacon Hill home and confronted him about his extramarital affairs, he threw her down the stairs and had her committed to the McLean Asylum for the Insane in Belmont, Mass. She tried to explain her predicament — that she was not crazy but was rather the victim of an abusive hus-

The grave of Phoebe Harris Phelps, foreground, a domestic violence victim who received assistance from Susan B. Anthony. She is the sister of Judge Ira Harris. At top, a detail of her gravestone.

PHOEBE HARRIS PHELPS: (1818-1889)

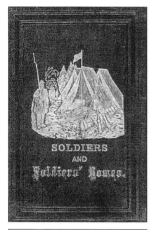

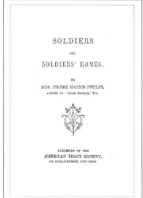

The Wood Sawyer lifting Little Delia over the Woodpile.

At left is the cover and title page of Phelps' book "Soldiers and Soliders' Homes." Above, an illustration from her children's book "Home Stories." This collection is dedicated to her daughter Delia.

band. But it was her word against a powerful politician and a medical doctor. She languished in the asylum for nearly 18 months and was not allowed any visits from family or friends. She eventually managed to prove her sanity and got herself released to the care of her brother, Ira, in Albany. Ira Harris was an Albany heavyweight: judge, state Assemblyman, U.S. senator, and president of Union College.

Phoebe's estranged husband tried to block her from visits with her children.

Frustrated, she sought the assistance of Susan B. Anthony, whom she met during a speaking engagement in Albany. Anthony was moved by her story and agreed to help Phoebe. Anthony helped Phoebe settle in Philadelphia, where she supported herself with sewing jobs and writing projects. She was the author of several books, including "School Stories, or Some Coats That Fit" (1863), "Mary Day's Story Book (Home Stories)" (1864) and "The Soldier's Ring, and Other Stories" (1865).

As Phoebe prepared to file for divorce, Anthony

helped her regain custody of her daughters. But Phelps hired security agents to track down and seize the children, and return them to his Boston home.

Phoebe died in 1889, a successful children's book author who had happily reunited with her grown daughters. She was buried in the Harris family plot, Section 18, Lot 3, off South Ridge Road.

When Phelps died in 1902 in Boston, his obituary mentioned his wife's name and nothing else about her. He was never charged with domestic violence.

STANFORD MAUSOLEUM (1795-1862)

BUILT FOR PARENTS OF RAILROAD MAGNATE LELAND STANFORD, CO-FOUNDER OF STANFORD UNIVERSITY

Josiah Stanford was born and raised in the area of Watervliet that is within the boundaries of the town of Colonie. He was a tavern keeper on the Schenectady road (portions of Washington and Central avenues today) that connected the frontier trading posts of Albany and Schenectady, originally a dirt path through the woods. As travelers and commerce increased along the road that linked the two cities, the Stanford fortune also rose and Josiah eventually became the proprietor of the Elm Grove Hotel in Roessleville, in the vicinity of Colonie Center today.

Josiah married Elizabeth Phillips and they had eight children, including six sons. They raised their family in Watervliet. The siblings gained renown and fortune in business and politics, but none achieved the prominence and immense wealth of the middle child, Leland, a lawyer who moved up the ranks of the Republican Party and became governor of California in 1861. That same year he became president of the Central Pacific Railroad and he exploited the nexus of business and politics.

In 1862, his father died. Leland built his parents a magnificent mausoleum in Section 18, Lot 105, not far from the spectacular monument he purchased for his wife's parents, the Lathrops, in Section 11. The Stanford crypt is built into a hillside on the lowlands, halfway up South Ridge Road, near a ravine overlooking the Moordanaers Kill, in the vicinity of the Volkert Petrus Douw crypt.

The Stanford mausoleum includes the remains of Leland's parents, three siblings and other relatives. It is an

Burial vault of Josiah and Elizabeth Phillips Stanford, the parents of railroad magnate Leland Stanford, who purchased this mausoleum and a monument nearby for his parents-in-law, the Lathrops. (Page 33)

STANFORD MAUSOLEUM: (1795-1862)

architectural gem with a formal staircase and gracefully curved wing walls of stone blocks, with a central arched portico topped by two carved urns. The mausoleum's substantial door is a cast-iron behemoth with filigree and detail work, dominated by capital letters spelling out the family name: STANFORD.

But by the year 2000, the mausoleum had fallen into disrepair and Eleanor Alter, a Stanford University alumna, was alarmed during a visit to the cemetery to see the family's crypt surrounded by yellow caution tape because the wall was so unstable it was in danger of collapse. Alter enlisted the assistance of Stanford historian Norman Tutorow and both appealed to Stanford President Gerhard Casper. An anonymous $100,000 donation to the university paid for the year-long restoration, supervised by the Stanford Planning Office and completed in 2005. The stones of the walls were removed and reset and the cast-iron was sandblasted and painted black.

More than a century earlier, Leland Stanford was elected president of the Southern Pacific Railroad and built the western portion of the first transcontinental railroad. Stanford famously drove the "golden spike" that connected the eastern and western portions in Promontory, Utah, on May 10, 1869.

The titan of industry was powerless to assuage the grief he and his wife, Jane Lathrop Stanford, of Albany, felt over the 1884 death of their only child, Leland Stanford Jr.,

Detail of the door to the burial vault of the Stanfords.

born when Leland was 44 years old. The boy died at 15 of typhoid fever in Florence, Italy, during the family's grand tour of Europe.

The grief-stricken father wanted to erect an epic monument and mausoleum — far larger than what he purchased for his father-in-law, Dyer Lathrop, or his parents — and he began negotiations with the trustees of Albany Rural Cemetery. But he wanted 350 acres, which was more than three-quarters of the cemetery's 467 acres and that much land was not available. Neither could Stanford's millions put together a parcel that large around his family's homestead in Watervliet (present-day Colonie).

As a result, the Capital Region missed out on its opportunity to become the home of Stanford University.

Stanford turned his attention to the open spaces out west and acquired property in Palo Alto, Calif., where he built his memorial to his dead son and christened it Leland Stanford Junior University in 1885. The couple endowed the school with $40 million (more than $1 billion today), which was three-quarters of the couple's estate. One of the first students was Herbert Hoover.

Leland Stanford died of heart disease June 21, 1893, at home in Palo Alto. After his death, his wife ran the university almost single-handedly, and her autocratic style angered trustees and created a cabal of conspirators who wanted her out. She died Feb. 28, 1905, in Honolulu. She was 76. Her death was long attributed to heart failure. The couple's remains were interred alongside their son in a spectacular mausoleum and chapel on the campus of Stanford University.

But the death of Jane Lathrop Stanford was actually a murder, and it was covered up in a conspiracy of university leaders, rarely mentioned and never fully examined until publication of a 2003 book by Stanford University Press, "The Mysterious Death of Jane Stanford," written by a Stanford physician, Dr. Robert W.P. Cutler. Cutler provided detailed medical evidence that proved that Jane Stanford was twice poisoned with strychnine. The first attempted murder failed on Jan. 14, 1905, at the Stanford mansion in the Nob Hill neighborhood of San Francisco, when she recovered from the poison. She died after a second poisoning in her room at the Moana Hotel in Honolulu. The only person present at both poisonings was her personal secretary, Bertha Berner, who took Jane a glass of water on both occasions. Berner was never prosecuted. In her will, Jane Stanford bequeathed a home and the equivalent of $100,000 in today's money to Berner.

GILBERT M. TUCKER JR. (1880-1968)

TITANIC SURVIVOR

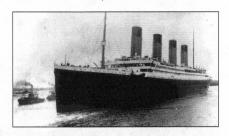

ilbert M. Tucker Jr. climbed into lifeboat No. 7 of the RMS Titanic with three female companions and a Pomeranian dog wrapped in a blanket.

The lifeboat was loaded with 12 women, 13 men and three crew members, and it was the first lifeboat lowered as the disabled British passenger liner took on water and slowly sank after colliding with an iceberg. It was about half-full.

The decision to take a seat in lifeboat No. 7 saved Tucker's life and gave him notoriety as a Titanic survivor. Tucker was one of 325 men who survived the April 15, 1912, catastrophe, while 1,509 people died, including 56 children and 114 women.

He spent the rest of his life carrying a heavy burden, trying to rationalize his survival while rebuffing rumors that he disguised himself as a woman to secure his spot in the lifeboat.

Back home in Albany, Tucker heard mocking whispers of "women and children first" as he walked the streets, which sometimes led to scuffles with tormentors.

Tucker grew up in a family of privilege. His grandfather and father published a successful agricultural magazine in Albany, Country

Grave marker for Titanic survivor Gilbert M. Tucker Jr. Above, the Titanic sets sail from England for its catastrophic voyage in 1912.

Gentleman. He graduated from Albany Academy in 1898 and Cornell University in 1901 before joining the family business as a writer and editor.

In 1912, he toured Europe with his parents, a family tradition. It was a working vacation where they conducted interviews and gathered material for a series of articles on farming practices abroad. During their travels, the Tuckers met a woman from Philadelphia, her daughter and her daughter's friend, Margaret Hays, a 24-year-old high school teacher from New York City. Gilbert, a 31-year-old bachelor, was smitten with Margaret and he began a courtship.

Gilbert was disappointed when Margaret and the other two women, along with their dog, prepared to book a ship passage back to the U.S. A

coal miners' strike in Britain and a coal shortage idled many passenger liners, but the women managed to secure tickets on the Titanic's maiden voyage. Tucker convinced his parents that he should change his travel plans and serve as their escort, because it was not prudent for the women to travel alone. He was elated that he would have more time alone with Margaret.

As lifeboat No. 7 was lowered chaotically 75 feet to the water, nearly tossing the passengers overboard, it took on water and passengers began to panic before crew members realized the drain plugs were not in. Tucker and the others saw the ship sink out of sight, accompanied by "screams too horrible for words," according to one of the women. After three hours in the lifeboat, they

GILBERT M. TUCKER: (1880-1968)

were rescued by the Car-
pathia.

Back in Albany, Hays
broke up with Tucker, and
at age 41, he married Mildred Stewart in 1922. The
couple had no children.
They lived for decades in a
6,000-square-foot 1830s
brick mansion and sprawl-
ing family estate in Glenmont called Rock Hill. The
Tuckers later moved to an
Arts & Crafts bungalow in
Pine Hills. In the 1960s, they
moved to California, where
they lived in an assisted living center in Carmel. Tucker
died in 1968, his wife in 1981.

"I never heard him say one
word about the Titanic," said
Norman Rice, 88, a longtime
trustee of Albany Rural
Cemetery and emeritus di-
rector of the Albany Institute
of History & Art. Rice dined
regularly with the Tuck-
ers, took dance lessons with
them, vacationed together in
Cape Cod and visited them
in California. "I didn't know
anything about him surviving the Titanic until after
he died."

Rice recalled Tucker as
a slight, soft-spoken and
well-dressed fellow who was
financially comfortable and
enjoyed a life of leisure. He
kept a small office with a secretary in the old D&H Building, now SUNY headquar-
ters, where he tracked his
investments, including early
shares of IBM stock that
performed spectacularly.

Tucker by midlife had
managed to put the Ti-
tanic infamy behind him.
He authored four books
and became a leading voice

The family plot includes the remains of Gilbert M.Tucker and his wife, Mildred.

for Georgists, a tax-reform
group based on the writings
of economist Henry George.
Tucker left his estate in two
trusts currently valued at
about $2 million to Albany
Academy, where the library
is named for his father,
Gilbert M. Tucker Sr. The
school has received funds
from the smaller trust and
the larger one was set up as
a life income beneficiary
instrument. Tucker stipu-
lated that two children of the
couple's longtime aides, who
are in their 60s and live on
the West Coast, will receive
interest disbursements until
they die. After their deaths,

the remaining assets will go
to Albany Academy, where
Tucker was a trustee. He described himself as a "devoted
son" of the school.

Tucker was cremated in
California and his remains
were interred next to his
wife's in the Tucker family
plot, Section 19, Lot 9, off
South Ridge Road overlooking the Moordanaers Kill. It
means "Murderer's Creek"
in Dutch. Tucker's granite
marker makes no mention of
the Titanic.

WILLIAM DALTON (1869-1968)

CHIEF ENGINEER OF AMERICAN LOCOMOTIVE CO. AND HOLDER OF SEVERAL PATENTS

W illiam Dalton lived in Schenectady and was chief engineer of the American Locomotive Co., known as ALCO. He was a consulting engineer to the General Electric Co. and the holder of several patents.

He also made a lasting contribution to the cemetery by commissioning noted architect Marcus T. Reynolds to design one of the most striking monuments in Albany Rural.

The cylindrical, columned and dome-topped white marble monument, known as the Dalton Cinerarium, is where the cremated ashes of members of the Dalton family are stored.

It looks like an ancient Greek celestial observatory and its classical elements possess an otherworldly power that draws visitors from across the cemetery to its peaceful setting in an open corner plot near the top of South Ridge Road.

Some observers have noted that the cylindrical cinerarium might also suggest a vertically set boiler of one of the great, powerful locomotives that Dalton helped create.

The Dalton Cinerarium is considered by experts to be one of Reynolds' finest classical designs, among numerous large-scale monuments he designed in the cemetery. It was commissioned in 1928, in response to the death that

The Dalton family cinerarium is located near South Ridge Road and was designed by noted Albany architect Marcus T. Reynolds (Page 44).

WILLIAM DALTON: (1869-1968)

year of Dalton's first wife, Ida Hill Dalton.

Dalton had previously hired Reynolds in 1910 to design a house for his family in Scotia, which still stands.

The year 1928 was a slow time for the Reynolds firm and the staff could spend extra time designing and redesigning the cinerarium's extraordinary details. It is built so that sunlight streaming through the oculus of the blue tile dome illuminates in a gauzy light an open book of marble with bronze tablets on which are etched the names of the Daltons whose ashes were placed beneath the marble floor.

Visitors can look through clear glass in a rounded, glazed bronze door with filigree set in the marble wall between two of the six ornately carved Corinthian columns.

An early estimate from the Vermont Marble Co. put the cost at $38,000, and Dalton forged ahead, despite the stock market crash of 1929.

Although he was an engineering innovator, he wanted the Dalton Cinerarium to mark him as a timeless hero devoted to antiquity.

Peering into the cinerarium, one can make out the names of nine Daltons, from William Dalton (1818-1899) to Philip Dalton Smith (1967-1995), described as an "ardent aviator."

An obituary revealed that the 28-year-old pilot, known as "Flip," grew up in Columbus, Ohio, started flying at 15 and became a United Airlines pilot who lived in Elk

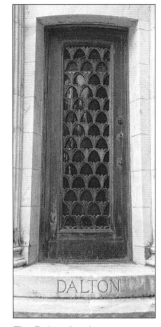

The Dalton family cinerarium, which was designed despite the 1929 stock market crash.

Grove, Ill. He logged more than 8,500 hours as a pilot and performed in air shows. His final purchase was a BT-13 World War II aircraft. He was flying that plane on Oct. 8, 1995, and performing aerobatics in front of a crowd of 3,000 at the Red Thunder Air Shows at Waukegan, Ill. As he tried to complete a loop, the plane's tail scraped the ground. The plane hit the runway on its belly and slid for a few seconds before bursting into flames. He was pronounced dead at the scene. He was survived by his parents, three sisters and six nieces and nephews.

As Smith had requested numerous times prior to his

death "just in case," on June 20, 1996, his parents sprinkled his ashes over the Philip Smith Mountains near the junction of the James Dalton Highway about 115 miles north of the Arctic Circle in northern Alaska. Some ashes were also placed in the Dalton Cinerarium.

His great-grandfather, William Dalton, who commissioned the cinerarium, grew up in Albany, attended public schools and graduated in 1890 from Cornell University with a degree in mechanical engineering. He came to Schenectady in 1894 and helped build the plant for the Schenectady Locomotive Works, later ALCO. He rose to become the company's chief engineer. During World War I, he was manager of the ALCO Ordnance plant in Providence, R.I. He retired in 1939 from ALCO and was also a consulting engineer at GE for many years.

He was active in civic life. He was a member of the original city planning commission in the early 1920s, was co-chairman of the Ellis Hospital building fund campaign in 1930, a trustee of Schenectady Savings Bank and a board member of the Schenectady YWCA and Schenectady County Historical Society.

Dalton remarried in 1929 to Sylvia Loines Dalton, a year after his first wife died, while the cinerarium in her memory was being built.

He died at age 98 in 1968 and had three sons, seven grandchildren and 14 great-grandchildren.

PRESIDENT CHESTER ALAN ARTHUR (1829-

21ST PRESIDENT OF THE UNITED STATES

There are dozens of congressmen, U.S. Senators, Cabinet officers, ambassadors, federal judges and politicians of every stripe buried at Albany Rural Cemetery, but there is only one president.

The tomb of Chester Alan Arthur (1829-1886), 21st president of the United States, is one of the most visited sites. He is perhaps the cemetery's greatest claim to fame.

The embrace of hometown boosterism clashes with assessments of historians, who consider Arthur's presidential accomplishments modest. They criticize his lax work schedule in the White House, extravagant entertaining, cronyism and tolerance for corruption. He was a stylish dandy, fond of sartorial flourishes, who rode about Washington in a luxurious horse-drawn landau with a liveried driver and footman.

Cartoonists lampooned him as "The Dude Presi-

dent." He kept 80 pairs of trousers in his wardrobe at the White House and often changed pants several times a day. A presidential assistant said, "He'd never do today what he could put off until tomorrow."

Arthur and his wife, Ellen "Nell" Lewis Herndon, a socialite from a prominent family, threw lavish and legendary parties at their Lexington Avenue townhouse in Manhattan.

But Albany Rural Cemetery historian and local au-

A bronze angel statue watches over the polished black granite sarcophagus of President Chester Alan Arthur. The grave is perhaps the cemetery's greatest claim to fame.

CHESTER ALAN ARTHUR: (1829-1886)

thor Peter Hess is a staunch defender of Arthur and his career, which included representing slaves pro bono in lawsuits and advocating equal rights for blacks, civil service reform and early support of the nation's maritime defenses that earned him a nickname, "Father of the American Navy."

Hess lashed out at a mocking 2006 White House Christmas ornament with a withering account of Arthur as a political hack that Hess called "an absolute disgrace" and "character assassination."

Arthur was born in Fairfield, Vt., on Oct. 5, 1829, the son of a minister. He was a tall and lumpish country boy when he arrived at Union College in Schenectady, but by the time he graduated in 1848 he sported extravagant muttonchops the size of apple turnovers and a bushy mustache. A classmate described him as "genial and very sociable" and "not a very diligent student." He was active in Union's debating society and was a member of Psi Upsilon with an affinity for gourmet food, cigars, billiards and fine liquors.

After graduating from Union, Arthur practiced law in New York City, was active in the formation of the Republican Party and during the Civil War served as quartermaster for the Union Army.

With a boost from Republican boss Roscoe Conkling, Arthur was appointed customs collector of the Port of New York, an influential po-

A Presidential seal detail on the grave of 21st President Arthur.

sition in which he controlled considerable patronage and graft at the Custom House. Arthur left the post under a cloud of corruption charges in 1878. Arthur's political clout earned him a nod as the vice-presidential candidate on the winning ticket with James A Garfield in 1880. President Garfield was assassinated in 1881 after just a few months in office, and Arthur became president to fill Garfield's unexpired term. A widower, he persuaded his sister, Mary Arthur McElroy of Albany, to perform duties as first lady and to help care for his daughter, Nell.

Arthur is enshrined in centrally located Section 24, Lot 8, in a family plot along South Ridge Road overlooking the Moordanaers Kill, one of two streams that cut deep ravines across the cemetery. The plot contains Arthur's wife, son, daughter, three sisters and his wife's mother. The plot is dominated by an imposing polished black granite sarcophagus on a dark granite base fronted by five stone steps and flanked

by a large bronze angel of sorrow placing atop the monument a palm leaf that has turned a rich aquamarine patina.

The memorial was dedicated on June 15, 1889, and was designed by noted sculptor Ephraim Keyser. Arthur's friends raised $10,000 for the cemetery monument and $25,000 for a statue of Arthur at Madison Square Park in New York City.

Each year, to commemorate Arthur's Oct. 5 birthday, a cadre of veterans places a fresh wreath at his tomb, sent annually by the current president. The cemetery applied for federal money to maintain Arthur's grave, but was denied because he is buried in a family-owned plot.

For many years, well into the 1980s, Arthur's late great-great- niece, Mary Arthur Doolittle, lived near the cemetery in Menands and was a frequent visitor to Section 24, Lot 8.

NORTH

ALBANY RURAL CEMETERY

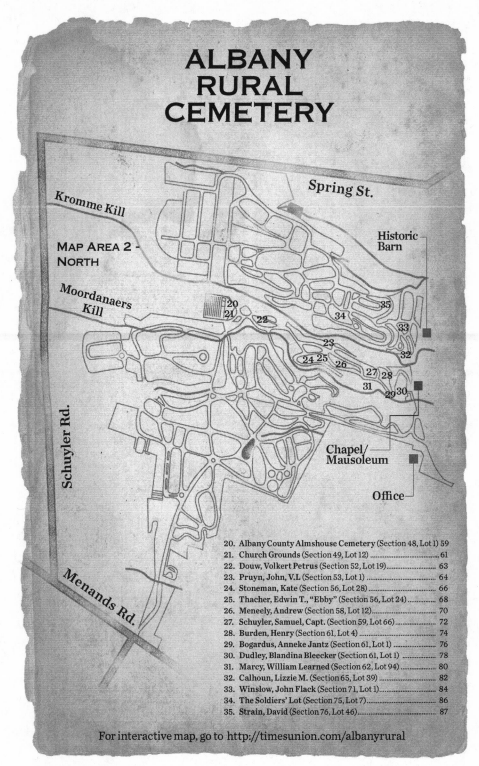

Spring St.

Kromme Kill

Map Area 2 - North

Moordanaers Kill

Historic Barn

20 21 22 34 35 33 32

23

24 25 26 27 28

31 29 30

Schuyler Rd.

Chapel/ Mausoleum

Office

Menands Rd.

For interactive map, go to http://timesunion.com/albanyrural

ALBANY COUNTY ALMSHOUSE CEMETERY (1896-1926)

FORGOTTEN POOR MOVED IN 2002

The Albany County Almshouse plot contains the full and partial remains of 1,125 people whose only crime was being poor.

They lived in misery, died without dignity and were buried in a potter's field off New Scotland Avenue in Albany, coffins stacked five or six deep in unmarked mass graves during the turn of the 20th century.

They were exhumed, moved and re-interred in Albany Rural Cemetery in 2002 at a cost of $2.4 million to make way for construction of a $60 million biomedical research facility on the University Heights campus behind the David Axelrod Institute of Public Health.

These nameless souls were considered the human detritus of the Industrial Age. Their ranks included amputees unable to work in factories, indigent single mothers with children they couldn't feed, the old and poor debilitated by disease, homeless, illiterate immigrants, the mentally ill and alcoholics.

At the almshouse, forced to do farm labor, men in their 40s died of exhaustion. Young women succumbed to cancer and consumption. Babies were stillborn or died from starvation and cholera.

It was a grim place. Researchers found that

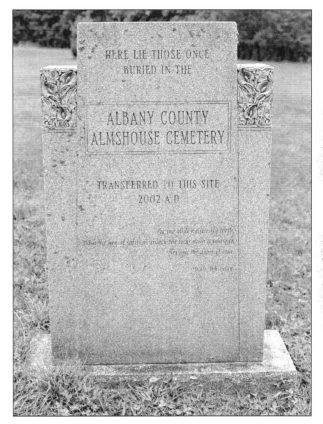

The Albany County Almshouse site contains the remains of 1,125 people whose only crime was being poor.

many men had fractured hand bones, injuries consistent with fistfights. Skulls showed broken noses or heads bashed in, legs fractured and ribs shattered.

Their research reveals a Dickensian underside of Albany history. Dutch colonists created the almshouse in the 17th century as a ware-

house for the marginalized and damaged. After several moves, the almshouse was located on New Scotland Avenue from 1880 until it closed in 1928.

Experts in the field of human osteology, the study of bones, are attempting to reclaim the histories of these unfortunate paupers, although records and maps were spotty and it is nearly impossible to match bones with names in century-old almshouse registers.

It is unclear if the remains of Mary Barker were dug up and re-interred. Her situation was not uncommon.

She emigrated in February 1871, from a farm in County Clare, Ireland, and, too sick to support herself, ended up in the almshouse. She died 10 months later of consumption. She was 45.

The almshouse cemetery was a catch-all for the indi-gent, including unidentified corpses found in the Hudson River, penitentiary inmates, street vagrants and new immigrants with no relatives.

Very few were buried with valuables. During exhumation, four rings, a half-dozen smoking pipes and a couple of rosaries were found.

In 2002, they were re-buried in individual caskets and vaults on a windswept, one-acre meadow on Section 48 near the intersection of Linden Avenue and Middle Ridge Road. Marginalized and anonymous in life, their final resting place is alongside Albany's Dutch ruling elite.

A five-foot gray granite monument reads: "Here lie those once buried in the Albany County Almshouse Cemetery."

There is a stanza from a Walt Whitman poem: "Let me glide noiselessly forth;/ With the key of softness unlock the locks with a whisper,/Set ope the doors o soul."

The other side bears a Latin phrase, Requiescat In Pace. Rest in peace.

A view of the front of the Albany County Almshouse, Jan. 18, 1932.

CHURCH GROUNDS (1868)

REMAINS MOVED FROM
ALBANY'S WASHINGTON PARK
IN 1868, INCLUDING FAMOUS
ARCHITECT PHILIP HOOKER

T he Church Grounds, also known as the Corporation Plot, contain the remains of untold thousands of Colonial-era city residents. They were reinterred in this isolated pocket of the cemetery after being removed from the State Street Burying Grounds on the northeastern edge of Washington Park near Albany's Willett Street.

The 1868 move was undertaken at a cost of $40,000 to the city, spurred by public health concerns, including possible well contamination, as well as the neglected condition of the urban cemetery and the allure of a romantic and sylvan setting championed by the rural cemetery movement of the 1840s.

There was also the practical matter of Albany developers who coveted the downtown cemetery land, prime real estate where they built fashionable row houses along the park.

This wholesale, large-scale removal of remains also underscored the fact that, even in death, religious affiliation divided a citizenry more than united it.

The 1868 reinterment was not the first time the bodies had been moved. The Washington Park cemetery was the third or fourth

Philip Hooker's grave stone, top, and an etching of the former Albany Academy building designed by architect Philip Hooker.

"final resting place" in some instances, as each downtown church — Dutch Reformed, Episcopal, Baptist, Roman Catholic and other denominations — outgrew small burying grounds. An outcry arose among congregants over coffins being stacked four or five deep. Also, flooding from heavy rains eroded the crowded cemeteries, opened coffins and scattered remains.

The city purchased thousands of simple pine coffins for the 1868 move, but there are no records at Albany Rural of how many people were reinterred and there is no way of knowing exactly who is buried where. The

cemetery trustees placed the Church Grounds in Section 49, Lot 12, at the top of Middle Ridge Road near the intersection of Linden Avenue. It abuts Jewish burial grounds, the Beth Emeth Cemetery, which purchased property from Albany Rural also in the late-1800s for burials of people of Jewish faith. The Catholic cemetery, Saint Agnes Cemetery, which borders Albany Rural on its southern edge, also received reinterred remains of Catholics in the move.

When the thousands of remains arrived in scores of horse-drawn wagons, they were reinterred as they had been arranged in

CHURCH GROUNDS: (1868)

Washington Park: Church by church, congregation by congregation. The plot is weedy and overgrown today. The few dozen gravestones that were moved to the site were inexplicably laid flat. This hastened weathering and has rendered nearly all of them illegible today. It is evident from contemporary newspaper accounts and the research of historians that they were placed in rows that resemble church pews: Reformed Dutch here, Episcopalians there, Baptists here, et cetera.

And in a forlorn corner along the tree line of the woods, African-Americans were reinterred together, members of the AME or African Methodist Episcopal Church. The AME section also includes several former slaves.

One gravestone in the AME section that can still be deciphered is that of Samuel Edge (1790-1846), who was born on the island of St. Croix in the West Indies circa 1790 and likely came to America as a slave. He was identified as a "free person of color" in city directories starting in 1813. He settled in Arbor Hill and worked as a janitor, shoemaker and hairdresser. He lived in Arbor Hill for four decades and was a prominent member of the city's free black community. He married Caty Arnold, a Lutheran, and owned property. He died in the fall of 1846.

Across the Church Grounds, in a place of prominence, the only gravestone placed upright belongs to

Grave stones that were relocated from Washington Park in 1868 to Albany Rural Cemetery.

Philip Hooker (1766-1836), one of the greatest architects in Albany's history. His simple white marble tombstone had fallen over and cracked, but it was recently repaired with mortar and returned to its original position.

Hooker was born and raised in Rutland, Mass., the son of a carpenter. At around age 6, he moved to Albany with his parents and seven siblings. He learned carpentry from his father and served the city as city architect, alderman, assessor and city surveyor. He was a singular force in the transformation of downtown Albany in the late-18th and early-19th centuries.

Hooker designed some of the most celebrated buildings in the city, including the original Albany Academy (1815), an elegant brownstone in Academy Park between City Hall and the Capitol that is the Albany school district's headquarters today. He also designed the original state Capitol (1809), at the head of the State Street Hill, demolished in 1883 to make way for a

new Capitol building. Hooker designed the previous City Hall (1829) on Eagle Street, which burned in 1880 and was demolished to make way for the H.H. Richardson design that stands today.

Dozens of Hooker's designs, regrettably, no longer exist, but among extant examples of his graceful aesthetic are the Fort Orange Club at 110 Washington Ave., originally a mansion he built for Samuel Hill; and the twin-spired North Dutch Reformed Church on North Pearl Street at Clinton Square, across from Capital Repertory Theatre. It is now known as First Church and a brass nameplate marks the pew where Teddy Roosevelt sat during services while he was a state assemblyman and governor living in Albany. His wife, Edith, and their children, however, attended the Episcopal All Saints' Cathedral across town.

Even the Roosevelt household, alas, underscored the faith divisions that led to the denominational segregation found in the 1868 Church Grounds.

VOLKERT PETRUS DOUW (1720-1801)

FOUNDING FATHER OF COLONIAL ALBANY, VICE-PRESIDENT OF FIRST PROVINCIAL CONGRESS

Volkert Petrus Douw was a founding father of Colonial Albany and a leading citizen of the 18th-century city who held its most trusted positions: vice-president of the First Provincial Congress, mayor, captain of the Colonial Militia, Indian commissioner, first judge of County Court and state senator.

Douw also has one of the creepiest crypts in the cemetery, a Dutch-style gray and brown stone vault built into a shaded slope in an out-of-the-way area. The location is so spookily evocative that it was chosen for a scene in the film version of William Kennedy's Pulitzer-winning novel "Ironweed." Francis Phelan, portrayed by Jack Nicholson, is hired as a grave digger with his buddy, Rudy, played by Tom Waits, and Phelan begins receiving messages from the dead.

Volkert Petrus Douw benefited from good connections. His father married into the city's most prominent family, the Van Rensselaers, descendants of the patroon. Volkert was the only surviving son of nine children born to Petrus and Anna Van Rensselaer Douw. As a young man, he worked in the family's store in downtown Albany and on the Douw

The hillside crypt of Volkert Petrus Douw. The crypt was featured in the film "Ironweed."

farm across the Hudson River in what is now the city of Rensselaer. They named their country estate Wolvenhook. He married Anna De Peyster at age 22. The couple had nine children, all baptized in the Dutch church where Volkert was appointed a church officer.

He worked as a Hudson River skipper and eventually returned to running the family store. By the 1750s, Douw was a pillar of the community, beginning as an alderman and member of the City Council. He moved up the ranks in politics. During the American Revolution, he was a member of the Albany Committee of Correspon-

dence, a delegate to the Provincial Congress and a commissioner and commissary to the Indians.

He was also one of the city's wealthiest residents, building a fortune through trade and export. A sign of his economic standing was that his household owned 14 slaves in 1790. He retired from the state Senate in 1793 and died at age 81 at Wolvenhook. He was buried in a family cemetery on the farm and his remains were moved years later to the distinctive Douw crypt, slotted into a hillside on Section 52, Lot 19, off Middle Ridge Road and hugging the low ground along the Moordanaers Kill.

JOHN V.L. PRUYN
(1797-1882)

LAWYER, CONGRESSMAN, REGENT AND CHANCELLOR OF SUNY

J ohn Van Schaick Lansing Pruyn began life with one of the most powerful, and prominent, old Dutch family names and enhanced his prestige by marrying the niece of iron magnate and railroad baron Erastus Corning. To call him well-connected was a gross understatement.

Pruyn took a traditional route to success. He graduated from Albany Academy in 1826, studied law and was admitted to the New York Bar in 1832, and started a law practice in Albany.

He married Corning's niece, Harriet Corning Turner, in 1840. They had six children and the two who lived to adulthood were John V.L. Pruyn Jr. and Erastus Corning Pruyn.

He worked closely with his wife's uncle since his legal skills paired well with Corning's business acumen, and the fortunes of both rose swiftly as Pruyn negotiated the contracts while Corning acquired and merged dozens of small rail lines into the New York Central Railroad.

His first wife died in 1859. He remarried, this time to Anna Fenn Parker, the daughter of Amasa J. Parker, a prominent lawyer and judge in Albany who became a judge on the state Supreme Court. The couple had two daughters, Harriet Langdon Pruyn and Hubertie Lansing Pruyn, who published a chatty memoir, "An Albany Girlhood."

Lansing pursued politics,

The grave of John V.L. Pruyn, a former member of Congress, regent and well-connected lawyer. A large granite cross and scrolls mark the familiy gravesite.

but lost his campaign for Congress in 1854. He settled for a seat in the state Senate in 1861. He donated his legislative salary to Albany's poor.

Pruyn finally got to Washington in 1863 by appointment, to fill the unexpired congressional term of Corning, who resigned due to poor health and pressing business matters, not to mention occasional clashes with President Abraham Lincoln. Candidate Lincoln turned Corning down after he offered to make Lincoln a $10,000-a-year general counsel of the railroad.

Pruyn served in the U.S. House of Representatives during the Civil War and was re-elected to a second term, which ended in 1869.

He resumed his law practice in Albany and became involved with civic affairs and philanthropy. He was commissioner for the construction of the state Capitol and helped lay the cornerstone. He was also president of the Albany Board of Charities and handled the trust work for his friend, Harmanus Bleecker, whose bequest included $80,000 for city projects.

Pruyn's son-in-law, William Gorham Rice, served as secretary to two governors, Grover Cleveland and David B. Hill, and was a noted authority on carillons. Rice wrote several books on the topic and was the chief adviser on the design and construction of the carillon in the bell tower of Albany's City Hall.

Pruyn also was appointed regent and chancellor of the

Carillon bells mark the graves of John V.L. Pruyn's daughter, Harriet Langdon Pruyn, and her husband, William Gorham Rice. Below, a closeup of the slogan on the base of the large cross.

State University of New York. He died in Clifton Springs, Ontario County, on Nov. 21, 1877, at age 66. He and his wives and family members are buried in the Pruyn plot in Section 53, Lot 1, halfway up Middle Ridge Road above a ravine overlooking the Kromme Kill. The plot is dominated by a large granite cross, carved scrolls and two bronze Meneely bells, examples of the artistry of Troy foundry owner Andrew Meneely (buried nearby, in Section 58).

The base of the cross that rises above Pruyn's monument is carved with a phrase: "Until the day break and the shadows flee away."

KATE STONEMAN
(1841-1925)

FIRST FEMALE ALBANY LAW GRADUATE,
FIRST WOMAN ADMITTED TO STATE BAR

Kate Stoneman was a trailblazer who broke new ground and made it possible for future generations of women to pursue careers as lawyers. Yet she was reviled rather than celebrated for breaking the gender barrier and becoming the first woman to pass the bar in New York state in 1885. Her application to practice law was denied because "her sex was against her," the court said.

"Before the Bar in Petticoats" fumed a headline in an Albany newspaper article that began: "A woman be a lawyer? Impossible! Monstrous! Surely there must be some mistake!"

Stoneman left her family farm in Busti, Chautauqua County, to attend the State Normal School (now University at Albany). After graduating in 1865, she was hired as a faculty member at the school and taught geography, drawing, penmanship and school law.

She helped form the Woman's Suffrage Society of Albany, became active in suffragist and temperance causes, and began studying law at night after being named executrix of her great aunt's estate. She continued to teach during the day and pored over law books on nights and weekends. After three years, she became the second woman to take the New York State bar examination (the other woman failed). She passed both writing and oral exams, but was

The area around the gravesite of Kate Stoneman on the south side of Section 56. Stoneman was the first female Albany Law School graduate and the first woman admitted to the NYS Bar.

KATE STONEMAN: (1841-1925)

denied admission to the bar because she was a woman and there was "no president," three state Supreme Court justices wrote.

Stoneman lobbied the Legislature and Gov. David B. Hill, who signed the law that removed gender qualifications from Section 56 of the Code of Civil Procedure.

She became the first woman admitted to the bar and enrolled at Albany Law School in 1896 at age 55. Two years later, she became the first woman to graduate from the school. "We humbly advise her to have just as few women clients as possible. They are troublesome," the Albany Law Journal wrote.

She continued to toil as a suffragist and lived to see New York's women vote for the first time as an Albany poll watcher in 1918. In 1994, Albany Law School celebrated its first Kate Stoneman

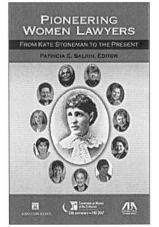

Day and in 2000 established a Kate Stoneman visiting professorship. She was inducted into the National Women's Hall of Fame in Seneca Falls in 2009.

She is the sister of Civil War General George Stoneman Jr., who successfully held off raids by Confederate forces at Chancellorsville,

Albany Law School in 1969 during a new wing dedication. Above, a detail of Stoneman's grave marker above and at left "Pioneering Women Lawyers" book that is part of Albany Law School's annual Kate Stoneman Day.

Va., and is immortalized in The Band's song, "The Night They Drove Old Dixie Down."

Never married, Stoneman is buried in a single plot next to a modest granite marker in Section 56, Lot 28.

EDWIN T. "EBBY" THACHER (1896-1966)

KEY FIGURE IN CREATION OF ALCOHOLICS ANONYMOUS

Edwin T. "Ebby" Thacher was an underachiever in a powerful, wealthy family of overachievers. He turned his lifelong struggle with alcoholism into a source of inspiration in the founding of Alcoholics Anonymous, a worldwide voluntary fellowship of men and women who meet to help each other achieve and maintain sobriety "one day at a time."

It was Thacher who introduced the principles of Jungian philosophy, spiritual values and self-examination that Bill Wilson, a friend of Thacher's since boyhood, used in devising the 12-Step program and co-founding Alcoholics Anonymous. There are currently an estimated 2 million members who meet in 114,000 AA groups in 170 countries. Thacher later became the AA sponsor of Wilson.

Wilson said of Thacher, "Ebby pushed ajar that great gate through which all in AA have since passed to find their freedom under God."

Thacher is revered for his role in helping millions of people around the world get sober since AA was founded in 1935. Thacher's out-of-the-way gravesite in Section 56, Lot 24, midway up Middle Ridge Road, is one of the most visited sites in the cemetery. AA members make pilgrimages to Thacher's grave and leave tokens of sobriety and other personal items, including notes and letters, to the man known as Ebby in AA circles, where the identities

The family plot where Edwin T. "Ebby" Thacher is buried. Thacher is credited with inspiring Bill Wilson, a longtime drinking buddy, to start Alcoholics Anonymous.

EDWIN T. "EBBY" THACHER: (1896-1966)

of members are kept private.

Thacher is the subject of a book, "Ebby: The Man Who Sponsored Bill W." He was portrayed by Gary Sinise in the 1989 TV movie, "My Name is Bill W."

Edwin Throckmorton Thacher was born into a family that amassed a great fortune as a railroad wheel manufacturer, and it also achieved prominence in politics, including three family members who were mayors of Albany. Ebby, the youngest of five brothers, did not measure up. He was failing academically at Albany Academy, and his parents moved him in 1912 to Burr and Burton Seminary, an independent, coeducational residential school in Manchester, Vt., that Wilson attended.

His parents moved Thacher back to Albany Academy after a year, because of academic trouble, but his grades did not improve, and it was determined he was not college material. He was given a low-level job at the family's factory. Thacher was drinking heavily by the time he turned 21, and within a short span in the 1920s both parents died, the family business folded and he lost most of his inheritance in the stock market crash. He had spiraled into alcoholism when he reconnected with his old chum Wilson, also an alcoholic. The two men went on epic drinking binges. By the time his older brother, John Boyd Thacher II, became mayor of Albany in 1926, Ebby's public inebriation had

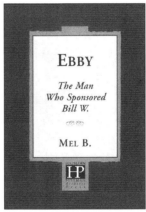

Detail, above, of Edwin T. "Ebby" Thacher's grave. The book cover to "Ebby: The Man Who Sponsored Bill W," by Mel B., of which Thacher is the subject.

become an embarrassment, and Ebby was encouraged to leave town. He ended up in Manchester, Vt., to be near his drinking buddy. Thacher ran afoul of the law and was arrested three times, including once after he crashed his

father's Packard into a house.

Thacher was visited by members of the Oxford Group, a fellowship whose members were devoted to sobriety and spirituality. In November 1934, he contacted Wilson and discussed the Oxford Group message at their historic meeting in which he is credited with "carrying the message to Bill" that sowed the seeds of AA.

Thacher lived with Wilson and Wilson's wife, Lois, for several months in Manchester until he got back on his feet and returned to Albany. Despite stretches of sobriety, he struggled with alcoholism the rest of his life and never fully embraced AA's 12-Step program. He was a heavy smoker and the effects of alcoholism and emphysema left him emaciated. He did not drink the last two years of his life, when he lived on a farm with friends outside Ballston Spa. He died of a stroke at age 69 in 1966 and is buried in the family plot.

ANDREW MENEELY
(1802-1851)

FOUNDER OF WORLD-RENOWNED
MENEELY BELL FOUNDRY

ndrew Meneely has a name and a sound that resonates across the centuries and across the Capital Region whenever church bells peal for Sunday services or the chimes of the carillon in the tower high atop Albany's City Hall pour forth crisp, ringing tones that can be heard miles away.

Meneely was one of the greatest bell makers in American history and founder of the world-class Meneely Bell Foundry in West Troy, known today as Watervliet. More than 65,000 bells under the Meneely brand were cast between 1826 and 1952, when the business closed.

Meneely was a silversmith by training, an alchemist who mastered the mix of copper, tin and molten heat to produce bells of elemental beauty and exceptional functionality.

The Meneely sound, revered for its rich tone and exceptional quality, can be heard in the carillons at Cornell University and Trinity College in Hartford, Conn., as well as at churches in locales as far-flung as Hawaii, Canada, Taiwan and Guatemala.

Meneely was born in Watervliet and, at age 15, left school to become an apprentice for Julius Hanks, whose father worked with Paul Revere, and Nancy Hanks, a relative, who was Abraham Lincoln's mother.

Meneely went into business with a son of Hanks, Horatio Hanks, and they

An obelisk marks the grave of Andrew Meneely, founder of the Meneely Bell Foundry in West Troy.

ANDREW MENEELY: (1802-1851)

moved to Auburn in Cayuga County in 1823 to operate a foundry that supplied equipment to the engineers of the Erie Canal. Three years later, after the canal was completed, Meneely returned to Watervliet to run a Hanks foundry there, which produced bells, clocks and engineering instruments.

Meneely married his mentor's niece, Philena Hanks. The couple had three children.

By 1836, Meneely put his name on the foundry and Meneely & Company became one of the largest and most acclaimed bell foundries in the country. Soon its reputation spread internationally. Its bells were loaded onto barges and ships on the Hudson River near the foundry and were sent around the world.

The bell casting business continued with Meneely's sons, Edwin and George. When a third brother, Clinton Hanks Meneely, returned from serving in the Union Army during the Civil War, his brothers did not invite him to join the family business. He started a competitor, the Clinton H. Meneely Foundry of Troy. They went to court and the two older brothers lost their lawsuit, which sought to prevent Clinton from using the Meneely name on his bells. The rival foundries continued in Watervliet and Troy and together they churned out nearly half the bells commissioned each year across the country.

Fortunately, the patriarch

Top, a church bell crafted by the Meneely company. Above, a detail of Andrew Meneely's grave marker at the cemetery.

did not live to witness his sons locked in a bitter fight. He died Oct. 14, 1851, in Troy. He was 49. He is buried in a family plot halfway up Mid-

dle Ridge Road, in Section 58, Lot 12, dominated by a plain marble obelisk, topped by an urn. There are no Meneely bells on the plot and no mention is made on the gravestones of the family's eminence as bell makers.

Incidentally, the 156-year-old bell in the cemetery's bell tower, on a hill just above the office, is a Meneely bell. In the early years of Albany Rural, it was tolled each time a horse-drawn funeral procession entered the grounds. It is rung only on special occasions now.

The life of Andrew Meneely brings to mind a poem, by John Donne, "No Man Is An Island," which concludes: "Any man's death diminishes me,/Because I am involved in mankind,/And therefore never send to know for whom the bell tolls;/It tolls for thee."

Capt. Samuel Schuyler (1781-1841)

Shipping company owner and early black entrepreneur

apt. Samuel Schuyler, a free African-American who came of age in Albany in the late-18th century, was a ship captain and successful entrepreneur of the Hudson River waterfront who became one of the early black community's leading lights. He was the patriarch of a large family with 11 children, and was revered as a pioneer of a slowly emerging black middle class in the city.

Known to scholars as "the black Schuylers," the provenance of the surname is unknown and no connection has ever been established with the white Schuylers, the family of Revolutionary War hero Gen. Phillip Schuyler, and the largest slave owner in Albany, with 13 slaves in 1790.

His house at 204 S. Pearl St. (near a Rite Aid Pharmacy today) was dwarfed by the Schuyler Mansion that looms high above on a nearby hill, a striking juxtaposition.

Samuel Schuyler started out as a dock worker, worked his way up to towboat operator and became the owner of a prosperous business he founded, Schuyler Tow Boat Line. Little was known and even less was written about Schuyler, neglected by newspapers and other recorders of the official history of the time because he was a black man. Most of 1,600 people of African ancestry who lived in Albany before 1800 were slaves, the property of an owner with no civil rights. They performed a range of

The grave of Capt. Samuel Schuyler, a prominent African-American businessman in Albany who died in 1842, is surrounded by more than a dozen stones of Schuyler descendants.

CAPT. SAMUEL SCHUYLER: (1781-1841)

jobs, were bought and sold and bequeathed as property in wills. They were dehumanized and as such were infrequently mentioned in the city's official documents.

Samuel Schuyler first showed up in Albany records in 1809 as a "free person of color." He and his sons, who took over the business in the 1820s, also owned and operated a flour and feed store and a coal yard. The family amassed considerable wealth.

The Schuylers were power brokers in the South End, the city's ethnic melting pot and the locus of the earliest black settlement in Albany after the American Revolution.

The best way to gauge the wealth and prestige of the black Schuylers is to visit their family plot along Middle Ridge Road, Section 59, Lot 66, on the high ground above the chapel with sweeping views. The location is among the most desirable in the cemetery, and in death the black Schuylers tower over the monuments of the adjacent white elite, including Gov. William Marcy and others.

ALBANY LINE
INDEPENDENT OPPOSITION.
Through without Landing.

The New and Splendid Steamer
Rip Van Winkle;
SAMUEL SCHUYLER, Commander.

Will run through the season, leaving the new Steamboat landing, (Broadway,) late Market street, on Tuesdays, Thursdays and Sundays.

SCHUYLER & Co.,
OLD LINE TOW BOATS,

Running on the Hudson, will leave New-York and Albany daily, for season 1848.

AGENTS.

THOS. SCHUYLER, 29 Quay-st., Albany.	JOHN SCHUYLER, 7 South st., N. York.

JAMES SCHUYLER.
COAL YARD,
CORNER FRANKLIN & BASSETT-STS.

All kinds of Coal in Lumps, Egg, Grate, or any other usual size, at wholesale or retail. Coal prepared expressly for family use.

Detail of Capt. Samuel Schuyler's grave marker. Above, an advertisement from a page of the 1845 Albany City Directory for Schuyler & Co.'s Old Line Tow Boats and Rip Van Winkle and Samuel's son James' coal business.

The captain's monument is a striking, 30-foot-tall obelisk of gray sandstone dominated by a large bas-relief of a ship's anchor and a letter S in ornate script. The patriarch's marker is surrounded by more than a dozen stone gravestones for Schuyler descendants.

The Schuylers underscore a story of industriousness, perseverance and overcoming racial discrimination.

Henry Burden (1791-1871)

Iron titan, horseshoe and rail spike innovator

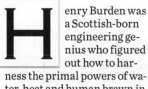

Henry Burden was a Scottish-born engineering genius who figured out how to harness the primal powers of water, heat and human brawn in order to bend iron to his will and to make himself rich.

His bitter rival, Erastus Corning, whom Burden sued over an iron manufacturing dispute, is buried on the other side of the cemetery atop a promontory in the largest single family plot on the grounds.

Burden died in 1871 at 80, Corning died in 1872 at 77, and even in death the

titans seem locked in a final struggle over who can lay claim to the most impressive final resting place.

Corning has prime real estate, but so does Burden, with an unobstructed view across the Hudson River to where he built his empire. Burden's large, ornately carved gray

granite mausoleum built into a slope is 10 times larger than Corning's lavish cathedral-shaped, copper-topped monument.

At least the feuding industrialists are separated by a few hundred acres in Albany Rural.

The founder of Burden Iron Works in Troy advanced the railroad industry a quantum leap and staked his claim as one of the progenitors of the military-industrial complex in the United States.

Burden's innovation was to dam and divert the flow of the Wynants Kill, a seemingly humble stream that

The Burden mausoleum contains the remains of iron industrialist Henry Burden. At top, carved stone dogs decorate the Burden mausoleum. At right, the Burden Iron Works and the site's open marble

Henry Burden: (1791-1871)

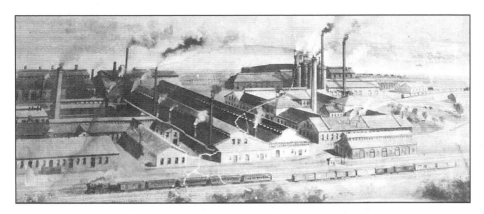

runs along South Troy before emptying into the Hudson River. (Burden sued Corning for tapping into the waterway.) He situated his Burden Water Wheel in 1851 at the bottom of the creek's 50-foot descent, a natural turbocharger, and built a stupendous apparatus that dwarfed competitors: 62 feet in diameter and 22 feet wide. It was a mechanical slingshot that pushed a veritable Niagara of extreme water pressure.

The water wheel drove his manufacturing plant, which churned out the first mass-produced horseshoes in the nation and achieved maximum throttle during the Civil War at a peak production of 60 shoes a minute, one every second, or 51 million a year. His annual horseshoe sales skyrocketed from $100,000 to $1.3 million in the war years.

The iron works was a Hades of productivity: 90,000 tons of coal burned yearly with 1,400 workers and a $500,000 payroll.

He was an Edison of mechanical engineering, with technologically advanced

rivet machines that could churn out 80 boiler bolts a minute and a rotary concentric squeezer apparatus that pushed out wrought iron as smoothly as toothpaste from a tube. The squeezer became an industry standard, as did Burden's hook-headed railroad spike machine that paved the way for a railroad boom in the U.S. — which Corning capitalized on, incidentally.

Burden's ego was matched by that of his wife, Helen, who designed the extravagant

vault on a plot where 22 Burdens are buried in Section 61, Lot 4, at the base of Middle Ridge Road near the Chapel. The site includes a larger-than-life open marble book mounted on a pedestal and carved with the voluminous Burden legacy. The crypt features a female face that resembles Helen, carved above the vault's arched doorway. But one's eye is drawn first to two life-sized dogs, beloved family pets, faithful retrievers that watch over the Burdens in perpetuity.

ANNEKE JANTZ
BOGARDUS (1605-1663)

OWNED 62 ACRES OF MANHATTAN

Anneke Jantz Bogardus was a Norwegian-born woman of modest means who inherited 62 acres on the island of Manhattan from her Dutch husband. It made her a widow of incalculable wealth in 17th-century New Netherland and the central figure in a classic rags-to-riches story that underscored the opportunities of the New World.

Their humble lives were also marked by high drama. A disputed land deed that gave the acreage to Trinity Church in Lower Manhattan, near today's World Trade Center, became a textbook legal case tied up in the state's courts for seven generations of Bogarduses across two centuries.

Anneke was one of the first and most famous women to settle in Dutch Colonial Albany. In 1623, when she was 18, she married a 21-year-old Norwegian seaman, Roelof Janszen. Neither could read or write and they indicated their signatures with special marks, which led to variations on the spellings of their names.

The young newlyweds were risk-takers and they took a chance as colonists for Kiliaen Van Rensselaer, a wealthy Amsterdam jewelry merchant and patroon who established the patroonship of Rensselaerswyck, a vast land holding that encompassed all of present-

The Bleecker family grave holds Dudley Observatory benefactor Blandina Bleecker Dudley (Page 78), and Anneke Jantz Bogardus, who once owned 62 acres of Manhattan in the Bouwerie.

day Albany and Rensselaer counties.

The couple and their two children arrived at Fort Orange in what is now downtown Albany on May 24, 1630, according to local records. Roelof was paid $72

a year as a farmer along the Hudson River near Normanskill Creek and he was appointed a schepen, or alderman. Anneke had two more children and the family interacted daily with local Native Americans with whom they

ANNEKE JANTZ BOGARDUS: (1605-1663)

traded. Incidentally, their daughter, Sara, later became the translator of New Netherland director-general Peter Stuyvesant in negotiations with local tribes.

In 1634, after the family paid off its contract to the patroon, they sought the bright lights of the big city and moved to Manhattan — "The Island at the Center of the World" in author Russell Shorto's memorable term — and worked on a Dutch West India Company bouwerie, the Dutch word for farm. That section of Manhattan became known as "The Bowery."

The industrious Roelof, who fathered six children with Anneke, was given a grant in 1636 for a 62-acre farm of his own near today's World Trade Center. The following year, he built a small house on the farm and his mother-in-law, the colony's midwife, lived with them. Roelof died suddenly in 1637 at age 35 and Anneke struggled financially as a widow, while the company refused to pay her 217 guilders she claimed her late husband was owed.

Anneke married again, in 1638, to the well-educated Domine Everardus Bogardus, who became minister of the Dutch Church on the lower tip of Manhattan. They lived on his wife's farm, which became known as "Domine's Bouwerie." The couple had four sons together and they clashed frequently with the colony's leaders on civic and legal matters, including the unpaid 217 guilders. When Anneke was widowed a second time at age 42, she had

Domine Everardus Bogardus, the second husband of Anneke Bogardus. At right, a detail of the Bleecker grave marker.

nine children to support and was cash-poor and land-rich with two farms — the second was 82 acres on Long Island from Bogardus.

Anneke moved back to Albany, then known as Beverwyck, and in 1652 she received a patent for a lot and a house near today's State and James streets downtown. As her children married and moved out, she gave each a wedding present of a bed and a milk cow. Her eccentricities and combativeness were accentuated and she was nicknamed "the vulture." Lore had it that she once hiked her skirts in a mooning retaliatory move against some heckling, pipe-smoking burghers she walked past. The incident wound up in court, a dispute that Anneke won by successfully arguing she had only been trying to keep the hem of her skirt out of the muddy lane.

Anneke died in 1663 after living for 16 years in Albany. Her will stipulated that her estate, including the 62-acre farm in The Bowery, be divided equally among her

seven surviving children. Her kids sold her Albany house that year to Dirk Wessels Ten Broeck for 1,000 guilders. The 62 acres allegedly was sold in 1671 by her heirs for "a valuable consideration," but the land was confiscated and turned over to the British crown after the English turned out the Dutch. The Brits leased the land to Trinity Church in 1697 for 60 bushels of wheat. In 1705, Queen Anne granted the land to the church.

By 1800, after swampy areas had been drained and commercial buildings were erected on it, the farm was considered the most valuable land in America. Today, it is some of the priciest real estate in the world and is worth billions.

Anneke's funeral was held at Albany's Old Church, built by her son, Jan, at the intersection of State Street and Broadway, and she was buried in the church cemetery. Her remains were moved to Albany Rural Cemetery in the mid-1800s.

BLANDINA BLEECKER DUDLEY (1783-1863)

BENEFACTOR OF DUDLEY OBSERVATORY

Blandina Bleecker Dudley reached for the stars and boldly went where no woman in 19th-century America had gone before.

The benefit of her philanthropy in terms of scientific understanding of the movement of stars was, in a word, astronomical.

Between the 1870s and 1950s, astronomers at the world-class Dudley Observatory accurately determined the positions and motions of more than 30,000 stars and produced two major reference works that became standard texts for stargazers around the globe.

Blandina was a descendant of early settlers, the Bleeckers, one of Albany's prominent Dutch families. Her British-born husband, Charles Edward Dudley, rose from Albany mayor in 1821 to state senator to U.S. senator. His political connections enhanced his career as a banker and he became president of the Mechanics' and Farmers' Bank in Albany. He died in 1841.

Widowed and childless, she donated a substantial portion of her husband's estate, more than $105,000 in the 1850s (roughly $3 million today). Her largesse created one of the earliest and most renowned observatories in the country as a memorial to her husband, who was fascinated by exploration of the night sky.

The Dudley Observatory was chartered by the state Legislature in 1852. The first observatory was built the following year on a hillside in North Albany. In 1857, an

The Bleecker family grave holds the remains of Dudley Observatory patroness Blandina Bleecker Dudley. Also interred there is Anneke Jantz Bogardus, (Page 76), who once owned 62 acres of downtown Manhattan in the Bouwerie.

BLANDINA BLEECKER DUDLEY: (1783-1863)

Above, a 1857 painting of the Dudley Observatory dedication by Tompkins H. Matteson that hangs at the Albany Institute of History & Art. Patroness Blandina Bleecker Dudley, who gave more than $150,000 to the observatory, can be seen sitting in the lower left. At right, a detail of Dudley's grave marker.

astronomer using a special telescopic device discovered a comet that was named for a donor and financial adviser to Blandina, Thomas Olcott.

In the early 1900s, the Dudley Observatory's research was supported by the Carnegie Institution of Washington and it operated a second facility in San Luis, Argentina. An early forerunner of the computer, an 1860s device known as the Scheutz difference engine, an astronomical calculator, is now housed in the permanent collection of the Smithsonian Institution.

The Dudley Observa-

tory churned along, aided by Blandina's $50,000 endowment, and relocated to Nott Terrace in Schenectady on the edge of the campus of Union College, with which the observatory was long affiliated. Its astronomers became world leaders in the

1960s and 1970s of the study of micrometeorites, tiny particles from outer space that streaked through the atmosphere and peppered the earth.

As technology advanced and the costs of astronomy soared, the Dudley Observatory changed its mission in 1976 from research to education. Recently, the organization merged with the Museum of Innovation and Science in Schnectady, or miSci, with transfer of Dudley's archives and historic telescopes nearly complete.

Blandina died in 1863 at 80, and she is immortalized in a marble bas-relief by noted sculptor Erastus Dow Palmer. She is buried in a family plot on Section 61, Lot 1 along Middle Ridge Road, with a soaring Gothic-style brownstone obelisk carved with her family's lineage, which includes the name of Anneke Jantz Bogardus, who once owned 62 acres in lower Manhattan.

WILLIAM LEARNED MARCY (1786-1857)

GOVERNOR, U.S. SENATOR, SECRETARY OF STATE, MOUNT MARCY

The towering legacy of American statesman William Learned Marcy is found in the name of the state's highest peak, 5,344-foot Mount Marcy in the Adirondack Mountains. Originally called Tahawus, a Native American name meaning "cloud splitter," it was named for Marcy who as governor authorized the survey that explored and documented the High Peaks region of the Adirondacks.

Marcy grew up on a farm in Sturbridge, Mass., graduated from Brown University in 1808 and became a lawyer in private practice in Troy. He fought in the War of 1812 and returned to the Collar City, where he got his start in politics as the city's first recorder and assistant mayor. He became state comptroller in 1823 and moved across the Hudson River to Albany. In the state Capitol, he allied himself with Samuel J. Tilden, Horatio Seymour, Martin Van Buren and others who formed a Democratic

Party "holy alliance" known as the Albany Regency, one of the earliest political machines in the country. After six years as comptroller, his political prominence led to his appointment as an associate justice of the state Supreme Court, followed by his election to the U.S. Senate. He returned from Washington, won his campaign for governor in 1833 and served three terms.

Marcy was the complete package as a politician: a keen legal mind, skilled at

William L. Marcy monument on Middle Ridge Road. Marcy, who had a keen legal mind, was also skilled at accounting and building alliances.

WILLIAM LEARNED MARCY: (1786-1857)

accounting and deft at building alliances. His tenure as governor was marked by pragmatism, efficiency and a lack of scandal. Those attributes led to his being tapped as a member of the Mexican Claims Commission in 1840, charged with investigating claims of U.S. citizens against Mexico. President James K. Polk appointed Marcy Secretary of War in 1845 and he was a top Cabinet official during the Mexican-American War. Marcy helped end the war by negotiating the 1848 treaty of Guadalupe Hidalgo, which called for the U.S. to take possession of the lands north of the Rio Grande for $15 million, assuming $3 million debt.

Although Marcy had never traveled outside the U.S. and lacked foreign policy experience, his reputation as a wise counsel and excellent negotiator led President Franklin Pierce to choose Marcy as his Secretary of State in 1853. He negotiated numerous treaties, including the 1853 Gadsen Purchase, in which the U.S. paid Mexico $10 million for 30,000 square miles of the country that later became part of Arizona and New Mexico. The tract made possible a southern transcontinental railroad.

Marcy also drafted the Ostend Manifesto, which laid out the rationale for a proposed American acquisition of Cuba. Public opinion and international reactions were overwhelmingly negative, which caused a chastened Pierce administration to drop the plan. Stung by criticism of the extent of slavery

The Benjamin Knower monument, near William Learned Marcy's grave site. Knower was the father-in-law of Marcy and a former New York State Treasurer. Below, a detail of the carved relief of Benjamin Knower fixed to his monument.

in U.S. expansion plans and conceding that it was trying to overreach as a new global power, Marcy bounced back by successfully negotiating a treaty with Great Britain over reciprocal fighting rights in Canada.

In all, he hammered out an astonishing 24 treaties in four years as Pierce's Secretary of State and he finished his service at the end of the president's term in March 1857. Exhausted, he returned to his home in Ballston Spa and died there four months later, at age 70, on July 4, 1857.

A New York Times obituary noted his life of public service and called Marcy "among the foremost men of the country."

A founder and board member of Albany Rural Cemetery, Marcy sold some of the land of his father-in-law

Benjamin Knower's estate to the cemetery. For his own plot, Marcy chose a scenic site atop the Middle Ridge, Section 62 in Lot 94, where he used to sit to enjoy the soothing sounds of a nearby waterfall and a sweeping vista of the Hudson River. Marcy's family commissioned the noted artist Erastus Dow Palmer to design his graceful monument, as solid and serious as the statesman.

LIZZIE M. CALHOUN (1858-1877)

ALBANY HIGH STUDENT KILLED IN CEMETERY CARRIAGE ACCIDENT

L izzie M. Calhoun was one of the brightest lights among 60 seniors in Albany High School's Class of 1877.

She was chosen valedictorian and was planning to deliver a commencement address at graduation in June of that year.

Calhoun lived at 7 Delaware Ave. and came from a prominent family. She was the niece of Albany County Supervisor James Young.

Her stepfather, Andrew R. Hunter, was a wealthy real estate owner.

The Albany Evening Journal said she was "one of the most loved and most promising pupils of the high school ... richly endowed physically and mentally."

On the afternoon of June 1, 1877, 19-year-old Calhoun and a friend, Alice Overton, took a carriage ride to Albany Rural Cemetery. James Clark, 21, who worked for Calhoun's stepfather, drove

The grave of Lizzie M. Calhoun at right. Calhoun died in the cemetery during a runaway horse accident on June 1, 1877. At top, the announcement of Calhoun's death in the Troy Daily Times.

LIZZIE M. CALHOUN: (1858-1877)

the two-seated carriage to "enjoy the invigoration of a drive through the bracing country air," the newspaper said.

Hunter had recently purchased the team of black horses that were "known to be somewhat restive and spirited."

The story continued, "The happy party entered the portals of the abode of the dead, little dreaming that hence one of them would never return alive."

At about four o'clock, while Clark guided the horses down the steep, curved North Ridge Road, the cross reins got caught up under the carriage. The horses were spooked and bolted. Clark jumped from the wagon and tried to untangle the reins, but he could not free them and was dragged behind the runaway carriage.

The young women panicked and Calhoun jumped. "She fell with a sickening thud to the graveled road and lay insensible and bleeding while the mad animals rushed on with the remaining occupant crouching in fear and momentarily expecting to be dashed to pieces, not daring to jump, the lack of which daring undoubtedly saved her life."

The horses crashed through trees, smashed the top of the carriage on a bridge and came to rest in the lot of stone carver James Gazeley behind the cemetery's chapel.

Clark and cemetery workers rushed to Calhoun's body "weltering in blood." They laid her on the grass

A detail of Lizzie M. Calhoun's grave marker at top. At left above, an announcement of Calhoun's merit roll honors as a freshman at Albany High School and an announcement, above right, of a Public Rhetorical Exercises program at the school. Both appeared in the Troy Daily Times newspaper.

and she died a few moments later. Her friend suffered a sprained ankle and a few bruises.

Calhoun's body was taken by carriage to her parents' house on Delaware Avenue. Gazeley carved her large, ornate headstone with formal columns and a bouquet of flowers. It is situated in Section 65, Lot 39.

John Flack Winslow
(1810-1892)

Iron and steel tycoon,
built Civil War ironclad Monitor

John Flack Winslow was a titan of the iron and steel industry, a partner of Erastus Corning and an engineering innovator who built the machinery, plating and other elements of the Civil War ironclad, the Monitor. He also was appointed president of Rensselaer Polytechnic Institute.

His fame and fortune are significant, but nothing in his resume looms as large as the Winslow Mortuary Chapel, the largest mausoleum among more than 40 in the cemetery. It denotes extraordinary power and prestige,

not to mention wealth.

The plot includes an approach of monumental staircases and three levels of terraces in order that Winslow's final resting place commands the highest point, with a view across the Hudson River of the spot where his iron and steel factories once belched plumes of profitable smoke.

The mausoleum is an architectural gem that resembles a Gothic cathedral, built of large blocks of gray granite, with a full copper roof, a large copper cupola and detailed carvings on its arches and dormers. It is visible from long distances,

with accommodations for 48 interments.

It looms high above the cemetery's historic Barn, just off Middle Ridge Road, in Section 71, Lot 1. It was built in 1864, at the height of the Civil War, and a 2009 restoration was paid for by descendants. The stone structure is the work of James Gazeley, whose stoneworks were near the Winslow plot. His company was one of the most prolific builders of monuments in the cemetery.

Winslow was born in Bennington, Vt., and his parents moved to Albany when John was 5. He left school at 17 to

The Winslow Mortuary Chapel is the largest burial structure in the cemetery.

JOHN FLACK WINSLOW: (1810-1892)

work as a store clerk downtown, took a job as an agent in a New York City commission house and at 21 left to work for New Jersey Iron Co. There, he gained broad knowledge of the iron manufacturing business. He had an entrepreneur's streak and in 1833 formed his own start-up company in New Jersey that produced pig iron. Four years later, he returned upstate to become a partner with Erastus Corning, who operated Albany Iron Works and later the Rensselaer Iron Works in Troy — the main rival to Troy's Burden Iron Works. (Henry Burden's large and ornate vault is not far from Winslow's, while Corning's family plot is on the other side of the cemetery.)

Winslow ran the day-to-day operations of the factory while Corning became preoccupied with acquiring small rail lines that would become the New York Central Railroad. Winslow had a gift for anticipating changes in the industry and he stayed ahead of the innovations, and his competitors. He traveled frequently to Europe to purchase rights to cutting-edge iron and steel processes. Corning made Winslow president of Lulworth Iron Co. in Mount Savage, Md., after Corning bought it.

In 1861, Winslow partnered with John Ericsson to build an ironclad warship for the Union Navy capable of defeating the Confederate's destructive ironclad, the Virginia. Under Winslow's direction, the machinery, plating and much of the other iron work for the Monitor

Rendering of the first battle fought between ironclad ships during the Civil War. Pictured are the Union's USS Monitor, bottom left, and the Confederacy's CSS Virginia.

were manufactured at Corning's factory in Troy. Ericsson created the revolving gun turret.

Frustrated by bureaucracy and delays by the Navy, Winslow decided to finance the $275,000 project himself. He technically owned the Monitor, which on March 9, 1862, at Hampton Roads, Va., defeated the Virginia, also known as the Merrimac, a ship that provided the ironclad's hull. After the stirring victory of the Monitor, newspapers proclaimed Winslow as "a benefactor of the nation."

In 1864, Winslow made the biggest deal of his storied career by purchasing the rights to manufacture and sell Bessemer Steel, a new British technique of producing stronger steel with fewer impurities. That same year, he commissioned the Winslow Mortuary Chapel in Albany Rural Cemetery — although he would not die for three decades.

Winslow was appointed president of RPI in 1865, the first leader of the engineer-

ing school who was not a minister. For the job, Winslow relocated to Troy from Poughkeepsie, where he was president of the Poughkeepsie and Eastern Railroad.

Winslow's first wife died in 1861 in the middle of the Monitor construction. They had no children. He remarried in 1876 and had two daughters, one of whom died as a young girl. The other married but had no children. Winslow adopted his nephew after his brother died. His nephew passed away at the age of 27 in 1877. He also adopted his second wife's nephew following his birth in 1883 in which the baby's mother died. That adopted son, Thomas Scudder Winslow, carried on the family name with three children and generations of descendants.

Winslow died March 10, 1892, in Poughkeepsie. He was 82. The cremated remains of several descendants are stored alongside the patriarch in Winslow Mortuary Chapel, the largest in the cemetery.

SOLDIERS' LOT (1862)

149 IDENTICAL MARBLE HEADSTONES FOR SOLDIERS KILLED IN THE CIVIL WAR

The Soldiers' Lot was created in June 1862, when trustees of Albany Rural Cemetery donated the .16-acre lot, near the bottom of North Ridge Road, Section 75, Lot 7, to the federal government for the purpose of burying Union Army soldiers of the Civil War from the Albany area. Most of the interments were soldiers who died while being treated for battlefield wounds or disease in the city's military hospitals after their broken bodies were sent by train from the South.

In all, 149 Civil War soldiers were buried in meticulously aligned rows of identical marble headstones. The last burial was in 1897.

The cemetery associa-tion's records noted the lot was donated with a resolution "that a sufficient and suitable ground be set apart to inter the remains of officers and soldiers who have fallen or may fall in endeavoring to suppress the present rebellion."

The lone monument in the stark and evocative plot, dappled by the shade of evergreens, is a 15-foot tall Grand Army of the Republic memorial on a large granite base. It was erected in 1873 and features a bas-relief of President Abraham Lincoln and a life-sized bronze statue of a Union Army soldier. Bronze plates bearing the names of the fallen soldiers are attached to its base. A total of 1,030 Civil War soldiers and sailors have been identified as buried in

the cemetery, based on the research of Civil War historian Michael Bodnar, including six Medal of Honor recipients, 26 generals and three Confederate soldiers. Most are buried in private family plots. Those in the Soldiers' Lot included many men whose families could not afford to bury them privately.

Over the decades, the ground settled and some gravestones shifted. A major restoration was completed in the fall of 2013. The marble gravestones once more stand in perfectly straight ranks as a stirring tribute to the Union soldiers who gave their lives to preserve the republic.

A bronze plaque marks the Soldiers' Lot. At top, memorial for the Grand Army of the Republic soldiers.

DAVID STRAIN
(1823-1844)

FIRST INTERMENT IN ALBANY RURAL CEMETERY

David Strain, who died at age 20 of consumption, a lung-related wasting disease that was common in the 19th century, would have been lost to the pages of history if not for the fact that he was the first interment in Albany Rural Cemetery.

He was buried in May 1845, several months after the cemetery was formally consecrated in 1844.

Little is known about David Strain. He was born on Oct. 27, 1823, and died on Oct. 24, 1844. He was the son of Joseph Strain, a soap and candle manufacturer.

There is a large marble obelisk that highlights the historic connection: "First interment and monument in this cemetary (sic)." Apparently, nobody noticed the misspelling or it was too late to correct it after stone carver John Dixon had finished his work. Dixon was the most prominent stone carver of his era and he did all his work by hand, with hammer and chisel.

Dixon is also buried in the cemetery, one of at least a dozen stone carvers whose best advertisements were the massive marble and granite monuments they created across its verdant acres.

David Strain is buried in a family plot shaded by tall oak and maple trees in

The burial monument and details images of the grave marker for David Strain.

Section 76, Lot 46, a serene and out-of-the-way corner off North Ridge Road, high above the cemetery's historic barn and the flatlands where the yards and workshops of stone carvers were located a century ago.

SOUTH

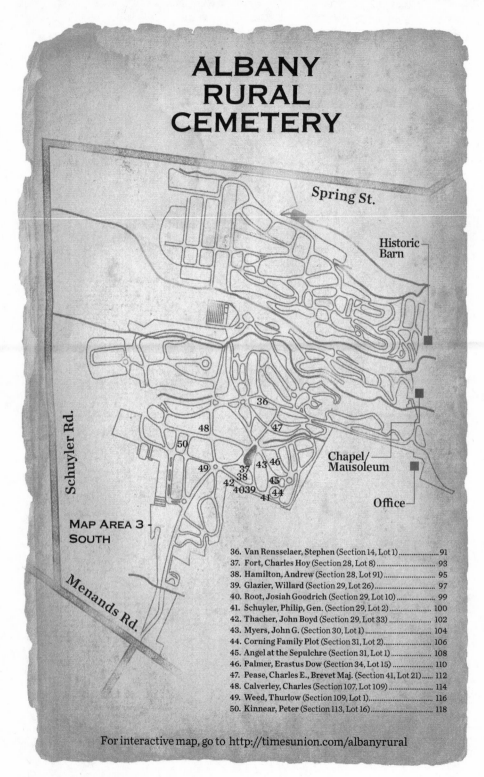

ALBANY RURAL CEMETERY

Spring St.

Historic Barn

Schuyler Rd.

36

48

50

47

49

37 43 46
38
42 45
40 39
41 44

Chapel/ Mausoleum

Office

MAP AREA 3 – SOUTH

Menands Rd.

For interactive map, go to http://timesunion.com/albanyrural

STEPHEN VAN RENSSELAER (1764-1839)

THE LAST PATROON, PHILANTHROPIST, FOUNDER OF RPI

tephen Van Rensselaer was the last patroon, the fifth and final Dutch patroon descended directly from the first land baron, Kiliaen Van Rensselaer, a wealthy Amsterdam jewel merchant who inherited as a boy the patroonship known as Rensselaerswyck, a vast tract of land that included all of present-day Albany and Rensselaer counties.

His descendant, Stephen, was well-liked by those who worked as tenant farmers in Rensselaerswyck and they gave him the nickname "the good patroon."

The Van Rensselaer family plot commands a large corner lot in the center of the cemetery, at the intersection of South Ridge Road and Cypress Avenue. The patriarch's elegant marble monument stands directly at the heart, designed by noted architect William Gray, surrounded by two dozen markers of family members arranged in a rectangle.

Van Rensselaer was born in New York City, the firstborn of Stephen Van Rensselaer II and Catharina Livingston. He grew up in baronial splendor at the family manor just north of Albany. His father died when Stephen was 5 and the will designated him, literally, as "Lord of the Manor." He graduated from Harvard in 1782 and married Margarita Schuyler, daughter of Gen. Philip Schuyler, uniting the two most prominent Dutch families in Albany. His father's will gave him ownership of Rensselaerswyck in 1784 at age 21.

Van Rensselaer's wife died in 1801, leaving him with three young children. The following year, he married Cornelia Patterson and she bore the patroon 10

The Van Rensselaer family plot. Stephen Van Rensselaer was a man of considerable wealth.

STEPHEN VAN RENSSELAER: (1764-1839)

more children.

Van Rensselaer did not have to hold any job, but he filled his days with public service and philanthropy. He was elected to numerous offices, including state assemblyman, senator, lieutenant governor, general of the state militia during the War of 1812 and member of Congress. He served four terms in the U.S. House of Representatives and was chairman of the powerful Committee on Agriculture. He was a congressman when he cast the historic, deciding vote for John Quincy Adams for president in 1825, giving Adams the edge over Andrew Jackson as the sixth president of the United States.

Van Rensselaer provided financial support to Amos Eaton and is credited with being a founder in 1824 of the Rensselaer School (Rensselaer Polytechnic Institute today), the first school of science and engineering in the country. He was the leading investor of the Mohawk & Hudson Railway and financed technological innovations in the industry. He also backed the planning of the Erie Canal and was the founder and first president of Albany Savings Bank.

Van Rensselaer oversaw more than 3,000 tenant farmers in Rensselaerswyck and he was widely regarded as a lenient landlord. Money was never a problem for Van Rensselaer, whose land holdings totaled more than half a million acres. When he died in 1839, his estate was valued at $10 million, which was calculated to be worth $68

Detail of Stephen Van Rensselaer's grave marker.

billion in today's dollars. The last patroon was buried in the family cemetery behind the Van Rensselaer Manor House, overlooking the Hudson River at Patroon's Creek, north of Albany, in what is an industrial stretch of Menands today.

During the 1840s, the mansion was extensively remodeled by Stephen Van Rensselaer IV and he lived there until his death in 1868. By the 1870s, the property was abandoned by the Van Rensselaers because the property was surrounded by factories, railroad yards and canal commerce. The family considered having the mansion relocated, but dropped the plan and it was dismantled in 1895. Prior to dismantling, the remains of the last patroon and other family members were exhumed from the estate and reinterred in the Van Rensselaer plot at Albany Rural.

Early cemetery maps show a stairway leading to an underground vault, but the stairs were long ago filled in and grass was planted over it. It is believed the remains of Van Rensselaer's father-in-

law, Gen. Philip Schuyler, the last patroon and other Van Rensselaers are in the long-lost vault. Cemetery trustees have discussed seeking permission from descendants of the family to excavate the vault in order to determine the undocumented contents. Nothing yet has come of those discussions.

The Van Rensselaer manor house was dismantled by architect Marcus T. Reynolds and partially reassembled on the campus of his alma mater, Williams College in Williamstown, Mass. It was named Van Rensselaer Hall and served as the Sigma Phi fraternity house. After fraternities were abolished in 1963, the building was used as a student residence and as the Center for Environmental Studies. It was demolished in 1973 to make room for the Sawyer Library.

The 18th-century entrance hall, considered by architectural historians as one of the grandest domestic spaces in Colonial America, was carefully removed from the building and donated to the Metropolitan Museum of Art in New York City.

CHARLES HOY FORT
(1874-1932)

AUTHOR, PUBLISHER AND BON VIVANT
WHO INSPIRED THE FORTEAN SOCIETY

harles Hoy Fort was a versatile thinker and philosopher, investigator of paranomal phenomena, witty skeptic, celebrated author and publisher of Fortean Times magazine in London. His eccentric and compelling writings spawned a cult following and an international organization called the Fortean Society.

Fort was called "a patron of cranks" who gathered a coterie of oddballs and iconoclasts. As a writer, he was a skilled satirist who punctured the pomposity of scientists. He lived his life with tongue firmly planted in cheek and a reverence for agnostic skepticism.

To this day, the online Fortean Times publishes weird and outlandish tabloid tales. A recent day's sampling: "Dinosaur porn, borscht-loving bear, goldfish boy, ghostly dating, Iowa Thunderbird sighting and bacon near-death experience."

Fort's present-day followers are an eccentric mix ranging from believers in UFOs and spontaneous human combustion to hardcore skeptics and devoted debunkers. They make regular pilgrimages from around the globe to Fort's grave site near Cypress Fountain. The Fortean Society folks have made claims over the years to otherworldly experiences in the cemetery, including an alleged sighting two decades ago of a Bigfoot-type creature that lumbered through the mysterious and deeply

Above, the family grave of Charles Hoy Fort. Fort wrote and researched on anomalous phenomena. His works were widely read and spawned the Fortean Society.

CHARLES HOY FORT: (1874-1932)

shaded ravines and stopped at Fort's grave.

Fort was an Albany native, descended from an old Dutch family. His father was a prosperous grocer and real estate speculator, and he grew up with two brothers on downtown's fashionable lower State Street in the late-19th century. Their mother died when they were young and their father moved them to a country home on the western edge of the city. Charles was the eldest of the Fort boys, who roamed the woods and became young naturalists collecting specimens of all types. They ran wild and became rowdy, contrarian teens with Charles as their ringleader. He clashed with his authoritarian father, who locked him out of the house and sent his unruly eldest boy to the basement's servant quarters.

Fort lighted out for New York City in his late teens, worked for a while at the New York World and then tapped a $25-a-month trust fund his grandfather left him to finance a world tour. He traveled on the cheap from New Orleans to South Africa, hopping trains, sleeping in fields and scavenging for food. He said he wanted to "put some capital in the bank of experience." After an adventure that spanned two years and 30,000 miles, he returned to Albany in 1894.

Two years later, he married British-born Anna Filing, a childhood sweetheart, and they settled in New York City. He wrote novels and worked as a freelance writer,

befriending author Theodore Dreiser and other literary lights including Booth Tarkington and Ben Hecht. Fort and his wife lived for many years in London, where he made a habit of rummaging through arcane archives of museums to gather more oddities. He wrote several best-selling books that are

The grave of Charles Hoy Fort and a detail of the marker.

still in print nearly a century later. His most famous work was "The Book of the Damned," an epic omnibus of the bizarre published in 1919.

So oddly powerful, hilarious and durable were Fort's writings that they spawned a counter-revolution by a group that calls itself anti-Forteans.

He contracted symptoms believed to be typhoid in 1932, shortly after completing his final book, "Wild Talents," which compared organized religion to witchcraft. The day he received a galley proof of the manuscript, he was taken to Royal Hospital in the Bronx and died there on May 3, 1932. He was buried in a family plot, Section 28, Lot 8.

ANDREW HAMILTON (1854-1908)

LAWYER, JUDGE, AUTHOR AND GRIEF-STRICKEN FATHER

Andrew Hamilton was the patriarch of a prominent family beset by tragedy. His only son died at age 7 of a childhood illness and, after he had passed away, his three grown daughters were killed in a train accident while returning from a funeral of a family friend in Hartford, Conn.

All the glory and heartache of the human condition endured by the Hamiltons was poured into the exquisitely detailed Celtic cross designed by famed architect Marcus T. Reynolds that dominates their family plot, Section 28, Lot 91, near the Cypress Fountain and across from "Millionaires' Row" of mausoleums near the intersection of Cypress and Linden avenues.

Every inch of the 20-foot tall obelisk and cross is encrusted with dense symbols that suggest modern-day hieroglyphics. It was carved by master sculptor John Francis Brines. There are traditional Christian icons, including a sacrificial lamb, Christ as the shepherd and an ancient pelican piercing its heart to feed its young.

Andrew Hamilton was born in Lansingburgh and attended Christian Brothers Academy and Albany Academy. He worked his way up from clerk at Western Union to a teacher, which allowed him to study law at night.

This immense and intricately carved stone monument is the centerpiece of the Hamilton family plot.

He was admitted to the New York Bar at age 21 and started a law practice with Hugh Reilly. In 1878, he married Jessie R. Walker, and she raised their three daughters as his law practice grew and he moved into politics.

In addition to his private practice, Hamilton was elected Albany City Court judge, Albany County district attorney and was appointed clerk of the state Court of Claims. He was the author of several legal textbooks and was a noted authority on corporate and insurance law. Hamilton was a former counsel to the

ANDREW HAMILTON: (1854-1908)

New York Life Insurance Co., whose business dealings were scrutinized by a legislative commission that investigated the insurance industry in 1905. The probe uncovered a slush fund used to lobby and bribe legislators on bills favorable to the insurance industry that became known as "the yellow dog fund." Hamilton was tied to the scandal. "The Judge," as he was known, made an impassioned defense of himself and the insurance industry before the legislative commission in the state Assembly chamber that took the heat off him and the scandal.

But mental exhaustion and poor health sidelined Hamilton, who never recovered from a string of losses: the death of his son in 1900, the death of his law partner Reilly in 1904 and the death of his wife in 1907. Hamilton died in 1908 of a heart attack while he slept. He was 54.

Four years later, on Oct. 4, 1912, the Springfield express train plunged down a 30-foot embankment near Westport, Conn., killing Hamilton's three daughters who were returning from the funeral of family friend Patrick Garvan in Hartford. Also killed was Mrs. E.P. Gavit, of Albany. Hamilton's daughters — Mary Hamilton, 27, of Albany; Elizabeth Hamilton Brady, 32, of New York City and Jessie Hamilton Ransom, 34, of Albany — were buried in the family plot two days later. Their markers are carved with the distinctive strap-work of the Celtic cross

on the monument.

Hamilton's daughter Elizabeth married James C. Brady, the son of Andrew Brady, one of the wealthiest New Yorkers in the 19th century. Brady amassed his fortune as an inventor and entrepreneur who owned a large gas utility and an electric streetcar company. His philanthropy included endowing Brady Maternity Hospital in Albany. Brady's

At top, a side view of Andrew Hamilton's children's headstones. Above and at left, details of the grave markers. A lamb is a symbol often used on markers to represent innocence and death of a child. Hamilton lost all four of his children.

son inherited much of his father's vast wealth, but according to newspaper accounts, Elizabeth Hamilton Brady endured a loveless marriage and expressed a deep unhappiness to friends at the time of her death.

WILLARD GLAZIER
(1841-1905)

CIVIL WAR CAPTAIN, POW,
EXPLORER, AUTHOR

Willard Glazier was the ultimate ironman and a peerless survivor. He lived by his sword and by his pen.

The quintessential self-made man grew up poor on a farm in St. Lawrence County and dropped out of school to make a living as a trapper in the wilds of the North Country. He saved enough to buy a horse and at 18 rode to Albany. He enrolled in 1859 at the State Normal School (now the University at Albany), with the intent of becoming a teacher. He ran out of money after a semester and had to leave, but he picked up temporary teaching jobs in rural Rensselaer County while periodically returning to college when he had enough cash.

In 1861, Glazier, most of his college classmates and two instructors enlisted in the Union Army. Since he had a horse, he was assigned to cavalry and the 2nd Regiment of New York.

He was taken prisoner Oct. 18, 1863, in a Civil War battle at Buckland Mills, Va. He escaped from confinement in Columbia, S.C,. was recaptured near Springfield, Ga., escaped again and with the help of several African-Americans, made his way safely back home to Albany.

Willard Glazier's impressive granite monument chronicles his life.

But his term of service had expired and he re-entered the Union Army as 1st lieutenant with the 26th New York Cavalry. He served with valor until the end of the war and was promoted to brevet general for "meritorious service."

He married Harriet Ayers of Cincinnati in 1868, an understanding wife who supported Glazier's unquench-

WILLARD GLAZIER: (1841-1905)

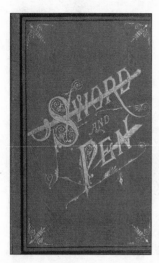

The book cover from "Sword and Pen," by Willard Glazier and an illustration of Glazier from his book "Headwaters of the Mississippi." Glazier was an avid explorer.

able wanderlust.

He transformed himself into an explorer and adventure travel writer. He rode a horse from Boston to San Francisco, beginning in 1875 and finishing a year later. He was captured by Native Americans in the Wyoming territory and escaped, which helped sell copies of his book, "Ocean to Ocean on Horseback."

In 1881, he set out to travel the entire 2,300-mile length of the Mississippi River by canoe. His adventures yielded two books and the discovery of what he considered the true source of the Mississippi. Although it was disputed as the source, Lake Glazier was named in his honor.

In addition, he organized a regiment for the Spanish-American War, had a river named for him after exploring uncharted territory on the Labrador peninsula, wrote several best-selling books and lectured around the U.S.

Glazier traveled a lot of hard miles and died at age 64 in 1905. His final resting place is among "Millionaires' Row," in Section 29, Lot 26,

and his large granite marker is strikingly visual: crossed swords, a bugle, canteen, a waving American flag and a long list of accomplishments that kept a stone carver's chisel ringing for days.

JOSIAH GOODRICH ROOT
(1801-1883)

COHOES TEXTILE TITAN AND BANK FOUNDER

J osiah Goodrich Root has a mausoleum as substantial and imposing as his name. It stands out for its size and grandeur and makes a statement even amid so-called "Millionaires' Row," a clutch of large mausoleums that is the most concentrated spot of conspicuous displays of wealth in the entire cemetery.

Root's mausoleum is made of large blocks of gray granite, fronted by a curved wall of polished granite and a formal stairway. The roof is topped by a large angel in white marble, with upturned face.

Root was born in Pittsfield, Mass., at the beginning of the 19th century. He left formal schooling early and went to work in a woolen mill, where he spent many years and developed a working knowledge of all aspects of the business. He married Martha Washington Meade.

He was tapped to start up a new mill in Watervliet in 1833 and managed the operation for three years before he was recruited by Stephen Van Rensselaer, known as the last patroon and one of the wealthiest men in the region, to run Van Rensselaer's Tivoli Woolen Mills in Albany. He worked for Van Rensselaer for several years before he struck out on his own. He set up a plant in Cohoes and amassed a fortune knitting

thermal underwear. In 1859, he opened Tivoli Knitting Mills in Cohoes and brought his two sons, Andrew and Samuel, into the family business, which he renamed J.G. Root & Sons.

The business prospered and in 1875 it became Root

The Root family mausoleum and a detail of the angel that sits on top. Root established Tivoli Mills in Cohoes. He was also a director of the National Bank of Cohoes.

Manufacturing Company, the pride of Cohoes and a huge financial success. The patriarch was in his mid-70s when he turned over day-to-day control of the company to his sons, but he remained active in the management of National Bank of Cohoes, which he founded.

Root and family members are interred in the grandiose mausoleum, Section 29, Lot 10.

GEN. PHILIP SCHUYLER (1733-1804)

REVOLUTIONARY WAR HERO, FATHER-IN-LAW OF ALEXANDER HAMILTON

P hilip Schuyler was a leading American statesman and a key general in the American Revolution who served at the pivotal Battle of Saratoga. He was named a representative to the first Continental Congress in Philadelphia and an adviser to Gen. George Washington, who stayed at Schuyler's mansion in Albany. Schuyler also was the father-in-law of Founding Father Alexander Hamilton, who married Schuyler's daughter, Elizabeth, at a 1780 ceremony in the Schuyler home, which is now a state historic site.

Gen. Schuyler's family plot, in Section 29, Lot 2, between the Millionaires' Row of mausoleums and the large Corning plot, is marked by a soaring column monument, surrounded by several marble markers for family members that line a border fence.

Schuyler was a homegrown hero. He grew up at the corner of State and South Pearl streets when the Dutch-settled beaver trading outpost was under British rule. His father and five other members of the Schuyler family served as Albany mayor.

In 1755, 22-year-old Schuyler accepted a commission as a provincial officer in the British army and he mar-

Burial monument of Gen. Philip Schuyler, major general in the Continental Army.

shaled troops at the military field grounds in the South End of the city, now called the "Pastures," and marched north on expeditions against the French during

the French and Indian War. After Gen. George Howe was killed in the disastrous British attack on the French-held Fort Ticonderoga in 1758, Schuyler transported the

GEN. PHILIP SCHUYLER: (1733-1804)

body of his friend and fellow officer back to Albany, where it was interred below St. Peter's Episcopal Church on lower State Street.

Schuyler was instrumental in the victory of the American colonists at the Battle of Saratoga in the fall of 1777, a turning point of the Revolutionary War. Residents of Albany, fearful that their city might be occupied by British soldiers, instead celebrated an unexpected victory at Saratoga. It was the first major win for the colonists and the residents of Albany rang church bells, fired cannons, roasted an ox and gathered around a large bonfire. Schuyler returned to the city of his birth as a hero and settled into his Georgian mansion. It was furnished in luxury by his wife, a member of the city's wealthiest family, the Van Rensselaers, who frequently entertained visiting dignitaries. The general enjoyed the life of a gentleman farmer and statesman on the 80-acre farmstead above the Hudson River. He served as a state senator in the late-1790s, but ill health and gout forced him to retire from politics.

Schuyler, who died in 1804 at age 71, was peripatetic after his passing. He was originally buried in a family crypt behind the mansion at 32 Catherine St. His remains were later removed to the family's burial grounds at its country farm and estate, Schuyler Flatts, along the Hudson River in Menands, north of Albany. Schuyler Flatts was frequently used

as an encampment spot for American troops. The farm and estate eventually fell into disrepair and the general's remains were moved to Albany Rural. According to sketchy records, Schuyler's remains were interred in a vault below the plot of his wife's family, the Van Rensselaers, Section 29, Lot 2.

Meanwhile, the large column marker was erected to the general in the Schuyler

Above, details of Gen. Philip Schuyler's burial monuments.

family plot, where 26 marble and sandstone tablets and three large table monuments were restored in 1999 with a donation by Janet Walker, a descendant of the Schuylers, one of Albany's oldest and most prominent Dutch families.

JOHN BOYD THACHER
(1847-1909)

RAIL CAR WHEEL MANUFACTURER,
MAYOR, SENATOR, DONATED LAND
FOR THACHER STATE PARK

John Boyd Thacher built a fortune as owner of Thacher Car Works, which manufactured wheels and underpinnings for railroad cars. He also had an important career in politics and used his wealth to build an exceptional collection of rare books and autographs. He also became a scholar of the life and explorations of Christopher Columbus. His widow donated 350 acres of land along the Helderberg escarpment that became John Boyd Thacher State Park.

Thacher was born in 1847 in Ballston Spa, son of George Thacher, who was mayor of Albany for two terms, including during the Civil War, when he hosted a visit by Abraham Lincoln's family and he welcomed an abolitionist convention in Albany led by Elizabeth Cady Stanton and Frederick Douglass. He started the rail car wheel company and built it up through a friendship with Albany railroad baron Erastus Corning.

His son, John Boyd Thacher, graduated from Williams College in 1869 and went to work at his father's foundry as an iron molder, one of the most difficult and demanding jobs. He learned the business from the furnace, and he took night classes in business management.

He found time to marry Emma Treadwell in 1872, and they had several children.

Thacher joined several civic associations, including the Albany Board of Health.

The John Boyd Thacher mausoleum, left, sits on Millionare's Row, a tribute to the rail car manufacturer, Albany mayor and philanthropist. His widow donated the land for John Boyd Thacher State Park.

JOHN BOYD THACHER: (1847-1909)

He worked to improve conditions for people who lived in the city's slums, which surrounded his foundry in the industrial section along the riverfront. He was elected to the state Senate as a Democrat in 1883 and shepherded legislation that aimed to curb the abuses of slum landords and to assist illiterate immigrants who lived in tenement housing. Thacher bucked strong opposition to pass an 1884 bill that allocated $1 million toward construction of a new state Capitol in Albany. He collaborated with Gov. Grover Cleveland to reform the spoils system and rampant patronage and corruption that flourished in Albany.

He left the state Legislature when he was elected mayor of Albany in 1886, a position held by his father and his son, John Boyd Thacher II.

While running his business and political affairs, Thacher found time to indulge his passion as a collector. He acquired valuable autographs, including all the signatures of the original signers of the Declaration of Independence. Part of his autograph collection is now housed in the Indiana University Library.

Thacher also was a serious researcher, who published articles and books on Shakespeare and Columbus, his favorite subject. His 535-page Columbus biography includes a table of Columbus' ancestors.

After Thacher died in 1909, more than 5,000 items of his vast collections were donated

Inside the Thacher mausoleum, at left. Above, a view of The Indian Ladder Trail at John Boyd Thacher State Park in Voorheesville.

to the Library of Congress.

Thacher was interred in a striking classical mausoleum amid Millionaires' Row, Section 29, Lot 33, along a colonnade of white marble mausoleums that resembles a latter-day version of the Acropolis of ancient Greece.

Thacher's crypt is subtly dedicated to his hero, the explorer. The rear of the mausoleum features a stained-glass window with a reproduction of the red Spanish Cross, similar to the one emblazoned on the sail of the explorer's lead ship, the Santa Maria. Observers have noted that Thacher, in death, sailed off into the unknown as his beloved explorer did four

centuries earlier.

His widow, Emma Treadwell Thacher, left a memorial in her husband's name far different than one of mortar and stone. In 1914, she donated 350 acres along the Helderberg escarpment to the state, with the stipulation that the land be used exclusively as a public park and a natural scenic reservation. Her husband had acquired the parcels many years earlier to preserve the area during a period of rampant limestone quarrying.

She, too, shared her husband's concern for conservation and humanitarianism. In 1920, she gave an additional 50 acres to the state along the west shore of Thompson's Lake, which became the state-owned Thompson's Lake State Campground. The Emma Treadwell Thacher Nature Center in the campground is named for her. She died in 1927.

JOHN G. MYERS
(1831-1901)

OWNER OF MYERS DEPARTMENT STORE

John G. Myers was a merchant who built one of Albany's most prosperous and iconic downtown department stores, and was hailed in his lifetime as a great businessman.

He died four years before his landmark store, a five-story structure at 39 N. Pearl St., collapsed and killed 13 people and injured 100. It was one of Albany's worst disasters. It occurred at 8:48 a.m. on Aug. 8, 1905, as 150 employees prepared for a 9 a.m. opening. The victims included 12-year-old Frank

Leonard, a "cash boy" who had worked at the store for just two weeks. His father rushed to the scene and dug frantically through the rubble, according to newspaper accounts.

The 100-foot-tall building — its back wall resting on jacks as part of a renovation project to enlarge the basement — pancaked down on itself and dropped the roof and all the floors and inventory in a twisted heap into the basement.

"Cries and moans of the victims under the mass of timber and brick appealing for help rent the air," said an

extra edition of the Albany Argus. "The most agonizing scenes were witnessed in the streets, where were gathered hundreds of the friends of the victims of the disaster, anxious for news of their loved ones."

Five miles north of the store, the Myers family plot is dominated by an eight-foot bronze angel, hands turned down in a symbol of sorrow, face cast in a dolorous expression. The angel and its dramatic wings have oxidized to a deep green patina. When it rains, the drops resemble tears as they run down the angel's face.

This eight-foot-tall bronze angel graces the burial site of department store owner John G. Myers and his wife, Mary. The monument is easily viewed from the Cypress Fountain.

JOHN G. MYERS: (1831-1901)

No mention is made of the department store tragedy. Myers and his wife, Mary Myers (1833-1904), are buried along with family members, their markers made of the same type of rose-tinted polished marble that forms the base of the angel sculpture.

The Myers family plot is situated along the edge of Cypress Fountain in Section 30, the lone survivor of seven ponds and lakes that were scattered around the cemetery a century ago. The fountain is broken and awaiting repair, but the still waters reflect the emotive power of the angel and striking fall foliage from large maples around the plot. The Cypress Fountain is a focal point of the South Ridge, and its benches are popular with visitors entering the south gate off Route 378 and Van Rensselaer Boulevard.

The 1905 catastrophe is largely forgotten today. At the time, so-called "disaster cards," postcards that showed a grim photograph of the store collapse, were popular collectibles. Investigators faulted the architect and builder for jacking up the wall on an unstable clay base, which caused temporary supports to buckle, setting off the deadly collapse. The report said about 20 minutes passed from the time the floors started to sag and some workers fled, but there was no formal evacuation of employees before the collapse. The report also noted that the department store was a mishmash of mid-19th-century wood-frame struc-

The John G. Myers Store collapsed Aug. 8, 1905, killing 13.

tures at 39 and 41 N. Pearl St. that were later connected, placing a heavy combined load and additional stress on the foundation. The interior was described as a warren of confusing, narrow hallways and staircases.

The builder and architect were taken into custody and fined, but there were no criminal indictments. The department store compensated the families of victims $1,500 from an insurance policy. One positive development was that public outrage over the collapse led the city to create a bureau of code enforcement.

The negative publicity caused some shoppers to stay away, but the Myers department store reopened at 37

N. Pearl St. and remained a longtime downtown commercial anchor along with Whitney's department store next door. The stores have been called "the Macy's and Gimbels of Albany."

After years of declining business downtown and the rise of suburban shopping malls, the Myers store closed in 1970. It was the last department store left in downtown Albany.

There was no mention of the collapse in a 1980 news story after an elderly woman was discovered prior to demolition, living "in primitive conditions" amid the rubble of the former store. An office building was erected on the site in 1984 and now houses several law firms.

CORNING FAMILY PLOT (1794-1872)

E rastus Corning, patriarch of the family that left a lasting mark on the history of Albany, created a template for more than a century of Corning conquests at the potent and profitable intersection of business and politics.

The Cornings own the largest family plot in the entire cemetery, situated atop the high ground of a long, sloping hillside with views across the Hudson River. This is the final resting place for five generations, including Erastus Corning

Corning family plot includes the graves of Erastus Corning, founder and president of the New York Central Railroad, and Erastus Corning 2nd, former longtime Albany mayor.

CORNING FAMILY PLOT: (1794-1872)

2nd (1909-1983), the 11-term mayor of Albany and the longest-tenured mayor of any city in America. The family's stature is embedded in one of the mayor's signature quotes: "I like being a big fish in a little pond."

Pale pink granite markers are arrayed in a gentle curve beneath the deep shade of a spectacular cucumber magnolia tree, a copper beech and other specimen trees planted by the mayor's wife, Elizabeth Platt Corning, a noted horticulturist who died in 1993 at age 81. The plot is dominated by a large cruciform granite sarcophagus topped with a bronze roof in commemoration of the patriarch. Its distinctive shape is an homage to the Episcopal Cathedral of All Saints in Albany, for which the Cornings donated the land and were major benefactors.

The original Erastus Corning (1794-1872) started as a proprietor of a small Albany hardware store and became a land speculator, iron magnate, entrepreneur, founder of the New York Central Railroad and one of the richest men in the state. He merged several small rail lines that stretched from Albany to Buffalo to form the New York Central, which was capitalized at $23 million in 1854. That made it the largest corporation in America at the time.

On the political front, he was also elected mayor of Albany, state senator and a congressman. He accomplished all these things

Albany Mayor Erastus Corning 2nd speaks before a crowd June 13, 1949.

and more, despite a major disability. A fall from his crib at age 2 severely injured his hip and spine and he was left hunched over and could walk only haltingly, supported by crutches.

During the Civil War, Corning's iron works in Troy won the contract to make the plates for the ironclad ship, The Monitor, and he profited handsomely throughout the conflict as a prime supplier of iron products for the Union Army.

The drive and ambition of the rail baron skipped a generation as his son, Erastus Corning Jr., burned through the family fortune in passionate pursuits: cultivating world-class orchids, breeding fast racehorses, rare breeds of cattle and collecting art and antiques.

Corning Jr.'s sons, Edwin and Parker, reclaimed the family's sterling stature in

business and politics and benefited from Groton and Yale connections. Parker was a seven-term congressman and a founder of Albany Felt Company (later Albany International). The extravagances he enjoyed included a chauffeur-driven limousine and uniformed house staff. He and his brother, Edwin, the mayor's father, president of Ludlum Steel in Watervliet, divided the family's 700-acre estate along the Normanskill Creek in Glenmont into the Upper Farm and Lower Farm, where each built substantial mansions. The Corning brothers met the O'Connell boys, South End ruffians, during illegal cockfights in Albany and forged a vaunted Democratic political machine that merged several strata of Albany's social and economic classes.

Corning's father was chairman of the state's Democratic Party and served as lieutenant governor under Al Smith. He was being groomed to become governor after Smith's presidential campaign in 1928, but Corning suffered a heart attack on the train heading back to Albany from New York City. Democratic leaders scrambled and tapped a young and little-known candidate to run for governor in Corning's place. They chose a state legislator from Dutchess County named Franklin Delano Roosevelt.

"Our family changed the course of history," Mayor Corning liked to say, with a wry smile.

ANGEL AT THE SEPULCHRE (1868)

BELOVED MONUMENT, ERASTUS DOW PALMER'S MASTERPIECE

Among the tens of thousands of markers and memorials in the cemetery, one of the most-visited, most-photographed and best-loved is the Angel at the Sepulchre, which is neither the largest nor the most ornate nor the most expensive.

The 7-foot white marble monument appears to glow and possess a magnetic qual-ity. There is an enigmatic aura to the seated, winged angelic male figure in a he-roic pose with palms resting on robed knees. Carved into its base are the words: "Why Seek Ye The Living Among The Dead." Critics consider it a masterpiece by renowned sculptor Erastus Dow Palmer, whose own substan-tial monument is located just down the hill.

It is situated in an unnum-bered, circular expanse of grass on a rise with an unfet-tered view of the Hudson River Valley. It commands attention.

The sculpture was com-missioned by Robert Lenox Banks, treasurer for the New York Central Railroad and a board member of the cemetery, as a memorial to his wife, Emma Rathbone Turner, who died at 31 in 1866. The famous angel

Angel at the Sepulchre, atop the grave of Emma Rathbone Turner on the south ridge is the work of sculptor Erastus Dow Palmer (Page 110). It was commissioned by Robert Lenox Banks.

ANGEL AT THE SEPULCHRE: (1868)

A hand-colored lithograph postcard from the early 1900s of the Angel at the Sepulchre. A detail of the Angel at the Sepulchre sculpture and the statues sculptor Erastus Dow Palmer.

sculpture drew art lovers from great distances and was featured on popular postcards from the early 1900s under the heading, "Greetings from Historic Albany."

A full-sized plaster model that Palmer created of his Angel at the Sepulchre in 1868 is a popular attraction in the permanent collection of the Albany Institute of History & Art. Many observers refer to the cemetery sculpture also as the Angel of the Sepulchre.

Preservationists are concerned of the effects of acid rain and weathering on the marble, including a damaged toe and a general dulling of the angel's features. An abrasive gray lichen has taken hold, hastening the decline. For years, the Rathbone family paid to have a temporary structure built over the sculpture each winter to protect it from snow and ice. The cover was removed in the spring. Eventually, the seasonal cover fell into disrepair and was discontinued. Suggestions to construct a seasonal, weather-resistant covering or year-round clear display case for the angel have gone unheeded.

ERASTUS DOW PALMER
(1817-1904)

SELF-TAUGHT, WORLD-RENOWNED SCULPTOR

E rastus Dow Palmer was working as a carpenter and joiner when he carved a likeness of his wife on a conch shell. He was in his late-20s and had caught lightning in a bottle.

His extraordinary talent was instantly obvious. Encouragement, commissions and drive carried him into the highest echelon of American sculptors.

Palmer has two sculptures in the U.S. Capitol in Washington, a statue of Philip Livingston and an allegorical sculpture titled "Peace in Bondage."

The sculptor's masterpiece, "the Angel at the Sepulchre," commands a hillside above his own stately monument, designed by noted Albany architect Marcus T. Reynolds.

Palmer grew up in Pompey, just south of Syracuse, the second of nine children in a large extended family that lived on his grandfather's farm. He married at 22 in 1839, but his wife and infant son died of an unnamed disease the following year. He married a second time, to Mary Jane Seamans of Utica, and supported his family as a carpenter.

He was nearly 30 by the time he earned his first commissions, for a series of small cameos carved on shells. In 1847, he moved to Albany in the hope of finding a larger market for his work. He

The grave of Albany sculptor Erastus Dow Palmer. Among Palmer's many works is the Angel at the Sepulchre, (Page 108), which is located not far from his grave on the top of the South Ridge.

ERASTUS DOW PALMER: (1817-1904)

moved beyond cameos and traveled frequently to New York City, where he mounted a major show of 12 sculptures for the National Academy of Art in 1856. He received rave reviews and larger commissions flowed his way. He commanded high prices for his busts of wealthy industrialists, including Erastus Corning and Henry Burden. Palmer's breakthrough was the full-length statue, White Captive, commissioned by Hamilton Fish and now in the permanent collection of the Metropolitan Museum of Art in New York City.

Palmer's studio and home were on Columbia Place, near Albany's City Hall, and he spent time at a farm in Glenmont, called Appledale. His artist friends included Frederick Church and two of Palmer's reliefs are on display at the Hudson River

School artist's home, Olana.

Palmer's son, Walter Launt Palmer, a noted landscape painter who won acclaim for his winter scenes, is buried in the family plot near his father in Section 34, Lot 15. Numerous works by

At top, a detail of Erastus Dow Palmer's grave, at left, his famous Angel At The Sepulchre sculpture; and above, the bronze relief of Thomas Worth Olcott on his grave marker on Middle Ridge Road.

both artists are included in the collections of the Albany Institute of History & Art.

BREVET MAJ. CHARLES E. PEASE (1838-1886)

CIVIL WAR COMMANDER, CARRIED LETTER OF SURRENDER BETWEEN LEE AND GRANT

Charles Elliott Pease was an Albany shopkeeper's son who enlisted in the 44th New York Infantry during the Civil War, survived numerous battles and close calls, was promoted up the ranks of military command and played a role in the surrender between Confederate Gen. Robert E. Lee and Union Gen. Ulysses S. Grant.

Pease's father owned the Excelsior Agricultural Works store at 84 State St. down-town and graduated from Albany Academy and Union College. In 1857, he joined the family business and learned the farming equipment trade.

In 1860, Pease was deeply moved by a dazzling display of military precision, drill formations and patriotism in Washington Park that was led by Col. Elmer Ellsworth and his U.S. Zouave Cadets. An Albany Zouave Cadets unit quickly formed, and Pease joined the outfit in the summer of 1861.

At age 23, Pease was

Brevet Maj. Charles E. Pease was a graduate of Albany Academy and Union College.

BREVET MAJ. CHARLES E. PEASE: (1838-1886)

appointed first lieutenant of Company G of the 44th New York Infantry while it was being organized. He fought with the 44th in the Battle of Centreville and the Siege of Yorktown. He was promoted to captain under Brig. Gen. James Van Alen of Kinderhook, and served as Van Alen's aide-de-camp. Pease later joined the Army of the Potomac and fought in the Battle of Gettysburg. For "faithful and meritorious service in the field," he was promoted to brevet major by Maj. Gen. George C. Meade on Dec. 6, 1864.

During the Appomattox Campaign's Battle of Hatcher's Run on Feb. 6, 1865, Pease nearly became a casualty. "My horse was shot under me and I had many narrow escapes," he wrote to Catherine Trotter, his girlfriend in Albany. "Was fighting six hours and have been in the saddle since daylight."

On the morning of April 9, 1865, a letter from Lee requesting a meeting with Grant and discussing terms of surrender arrived at Meade's camp. The major general told Pease to ride his fresh, new black stallion as quickly as possible and to relay the letter to Grant. Pease reached Grant 12 miles away, gave him the letter and rode with Grant to the Appomattox Court House and the Wilmer McLean house, chosen as the site of the surrender. Pease was told to wait outside while Lee and Grant conferred inside.

After Lee signed the document of surrender, he stood

The Appomattox Court House and Wilmer McLean house in Virginia, where the Civil War armistice was signed. At left, Gen. Ulysses S. Grant and Gen. Robert E. Lee.

on the porch of McLean's house and waited for his horse, Traveler. Grant told Pease to provide a military escort for Lee and his staff back to Lee's headquarters.

Pease resigned from the Army a few days later, returned to Albany and married Catherine "Kitty" Trotter. In 1866, Pease was hired by the Universal Life Insurance Co., and the couple moved to New York City. Two years later, their daughter, Estelle Cuyler Pease, died of chicken pox. She was 15 months old. They had no more children.

Pease died of diabetes at age 48 on March 25, 1886, in New York City. His wife buried her husband alongside their daughter in Section 41, Lot 21, off Cypress Avenue near South Ridge Road. He has a simple gray granite marker that makes no mention of his Civil War service. His wife died in 1897 and was buried in the family plot.

CHARLES CALVERLEY
(1833-1914)

STONE CUTTER TO ACCLAIMED SCULPTOR

C harles Calverley possessed of a strong work ethic, iron will and artistic ambition, climbed his way up from the lowest rank of a $1-a-week apprentice stone cutter in Albany to fame and fortune as a sculptor with a large studio in New York City. His work is in the permanent collection of the Metropolitan Museum of Art in Manhattan and Albany's Washington Park in the form of the life-sized bronze statue of Scottish poet Robert Burns.

Calverley was born in Albany. His father, a carpenter and machinist, died at age 43. Charles had to drop out of school at 13 and go to work to help his mother support his four younger siblings. He began a seven-year apprentice with local stonecutter John Dixon in what Calverley called "a one-horse marble shop." He worked hard and earned gradual raises and additional responsibility for creating marble mantelpieces, cornices, lintels and cemetery headstones that were Dixon's stock-in-trade. Calverley learned from a master stone carver who worked on the Capitol and City Hall in Albany.

Noted neoclassical

The self-styled bust of Albany sculptor and stone cutter Charles Calverley graces the family grave.

CHARLES CALVERLEY: (1833-1914)

Albany sculptor Erastus Dow Palmer noticed Calverley's exceptional skill and recruited him away from Dixon's marble operation at age 20. Calverley worked for Palmer in his Albany studio from 1853 to 1868 and specialized in ornate, artistic stone carving on memorial statues, busts and bas-reliefs.

Calverley left Palmer's employ and opened a studio in New York City in 1869, where he carved a bust of Abraham Lincoln that gained wide attention. He was inducted as a member of the National Academy of Design in 1874 and gained renown for his medallions and bas-reliefs of notable Americans, including George Washington.

Over the course of a productive career, he created dozens of works, including large monuments for Green-Wood Cemetery in Brooklyn and Albany Rural Cemetery. In 1879, he was commissioned to create a bust for Sen. Lafayette Foster, which is on permanent display in the U.S. Capitol in Washington.

A biography of Calverley, "From Stonecutter to Sculptor," by Elizabeth K. Allen, was published in 1996 by SUNY Press and the Albany Institute of History, which has several of Calverley's works in its collection.

Calverley's monument is the only one in the cemetery that features a full-sized bronze bust, which was made by the artist 20 years before his death. Calverley also created bronze bas-reliefs of his wife, mother and brother

Charles Calverley created the bronze statue Meditation, top, cast in 1902 when the sculptor was 70. It adorns Dr. Jepha Boulware's monument. The bronze angel, bottom left, marks the grave of John G. and Mary Myers (Page 104).

that adorn the family plot.

The bust of Calverley was stolen about 20 years ago, but a person who jogged regularly in the cemetery spotted it in a New York City antique shop and alerted authorities. The Calverley bust was recovered and was anchored more securely atop the artist's monument in Section 107, Lot 109.

THURLOW WEED
(1797-1882)

REPUBLICAN BOSS, LINCOLN ADVISER, NEWSPAPER PUBLISHER

T hurlow Weed was graced with a great name for politics. It was hard to forget and commanded attention.

He was a political power broker in Albany and Washington, a close friend of William Seward and adviser to President Abraham Lincoln. Weed was given several nicknames, including "The Dictator" and "The Wizard of the Lobby." He was a Whig and an architect of the Republican Party who later edited and published an influential GOP mouthpiece, the Albany Evening Journal.

He was one of the first to exploit the nexus of journalism and politics.

Weed grew up poor on a farm in Greene County and his father spent time in debtors' prison. With only a few years of schooling in Catskill, he left to work as a blacksmith's apprentice and earned 6 cents a day. At 9, he shipped out as a cabin boy on a Hudson River sloop. He could finally afford to buy his first pair of shoes.

After military service in the War of 1812, he settled in Albany and plied his printer trade at local shops and newspapers and in 1817, at age 20, he became press foreman at the Albany Register. He filled in writing editorials and was good at it. The next year, he married Catherine Ostrander of Coo-

The grave of Thurlow Weed in Section 109 off Linden Avenue.

perstown and failed in his attempts to start a newspaper in Chenango County. He backed candidates DeWitt Clinton and John Quincy Adams and was rewarded for his support. He parlayed those connections into a seat in the state Assembly in 1825. After re-election to a second term, he established

the Albany Evening Journal in 1830.

Weed had a disarming charm and was a skilled manipulator behind the scenes. He established his GOP bona fides by battling Martin Van Buren's Democratic machine, the Albany Regency, and relished a tussle with the Democratic paper, the

THURLOW WEED: (1797-1882)

Albany Argus.

He leveraged his friendship with Secretary of State Seward and elbowed his way into the role of confidant to Lincoln, who sent him as an emissary to Britain and France to urge those countries not to support the Confederacy during the Civil War.

Seward and Weed persuaded Lincoln to donate the president's handwritten draft of the Emancipation Proclamation to the Albany Army Relief Bazaar for a fundraising raffle in February 1864 that purchased medicine and supplies for sick and wounded Union soldiers. The draft E.P., as it is known, survived the 1911 Capitol fire and is the most important holding in the State Library. It is preserved in a secure glass case, stored in a vault and occasionally

Thurlow Weed used his political connections to become a confidant to President Abraham Lincoln.

put on display in the Capitol.

The Weed family plot, located on a prominent corner along Linden Avenue in Section 109, Lot 1, is dominated by a towering gray granite obelisk. The name of Weed's grandson is also chiseled into the marker. William "Billy" Barnes inherited the Albany Evening Journal and was the boss of a Republican political machine unseated by the

Democratic O'Connell-Corning organization in 1921. He commissioned an extravagant octagonal south tower addition to the D&H Building on Broadway at the foot of State Street (now SUNY Central). He hired his friend, architect Marcus T. Reynolds, to design a newspaper office and living quarters. His fortune crashed and he sold the paper in 1924.

PETER KINNEAR
(1822-1913)

Peter Kinnear took a small machine shop in the city's South End, teamed with a brilliant printer-turned-inventor and built a prosperous company that revolutionized the game of billiards and in the process eased the need for ivory hunters to kill elephants.

Billiards began in the 1600s using wooden balls, which were later made out of ivory, the preferred material for two centuries. The rising popularity of the game caused elephants to be slaughtered at an alarming rate and eventually caused the majestic species to become endangered.

In 1868, Kinnear joined forces with Albany inventor John Wesley Hyatt, who the next year patented the first commercially viable method of producing solid, stable nitrocellulose, also known as celluloid, which was the first mass-produced plastic. Kinnear was an early investor and invited Hyatt to use his machine shop to conduct experiments and develop prototypes.

Kinnear saw the potential of celluloid as a substitute for the declining supply of ivory.

He became the majority owner of the Albany Billiard Ball Company, moved the business into a large plant on Delaware Avenue at Southern Boulevard and developed molds and a streamlined process that could mass-produce billiard balls. He soon cornered the market.

The composition balls of Albany Billiard were more durable, rolled more uniformly and had a stable center of gravity that made them superior to ivory balls. The plastic composite balls were also less than half the price of ivory.

The manufacturing

Peter Kinnear's gray granite monument is surrounded by a dozen grave stones of family members.

PETER KINNEAR: (1822-1913)

At top left, celluloid inventor John Wesley Hyatt, 1837-1920, of the Albany Billiard Ball Company. Above, Charlotte Stadler worked on the line at the billiard ball company, January 1978.

process began with "gun cotton" ground to a fine pulp and combined with chemicals, formed in a mold and placed under pressure for an extended period to create a dense, durable ball that was perfectly round. The composite balls also did not crack, chip or fade like ivory.

It took three months from the beginning of the molding process until the ball was fully cured and could be shipped. The nature of the materials and the molding pressure made it volatile during production and there were occasionally explosions on the assembly line. Urban legends arose that claimed Albany Billiard balls sometimes exploded during aggressive shots, but there is no documentation of such occurrences.

The Albany Billiard Ball Company was an industry leader for more than a century and kept innovating with synthetic materials and plastic compounds to continue to improve the product and eventually switched to high-tech resins. Cheap imports cut into the Albany firm's market share, but it hung on as others went out of business and the Albany Billiard Ball Company was the last remaining U.S. billiard

ball manufacturer when it folded in 1986.

Kinnear's founding partner, Hyatt, formed the Albany Dental Plate Company and used his plastic innovation to produce false teeth and piano keys. His invention also revolutionized the manufacture of photographic film.

Kinnear became a civic leader and real estate developer and was president of the St. Andrew's Society, an Albany fraternal organization

founded by Scots in 1803. Kinnear lived in a Queen Anne house at 731 Madison Ave., near Washington Park, and led the effort to place an exquisite life-sized bronze statue of Scottish poet Robert Burns in the park.

Kinnear's monument is a large, plain rectangle of gray granite with a bronze plate that reads: "I Live In Hope." A dozen simple grave stones of family members form a necklace around the patriarch in Section 113, Lot 16.

ABOUT THE AUTHORS

Photographer Will Waldron, left, and writer Paul Grondahl at Albany Rural.

PAUL GRONDAHL

Paul Grondahl has been a reporter at the Times Union since 1984, where his assignments have taken him from the Arctic to Antarctica, and from Northern Ireland to sub-Saharan Africa. His in-depth series have won local, state and national awards for writing and reporting. He is the author of several books, including political biographies of Mayor Erastus Corning 2nd and Teddy Roosevelt's early political career in Albany.

WILL WALDRON

Will Waldron is photo editor of the Times Union, where he has worked since 1999. A native of the United Kingdom, he became an American citizen after moving to the U.S. with his parents in 1983. He studied photography at the Art Institute of Pittsburgh and at Pennsylvania State University. He has covered major news events throughout the United States, with his work honored in state and national contests and featured in several group shows.

THESE EXALTED ACRES
Unlocking the Secrets of
Albany Rural Cemetery

PROJECT EDITORS
Joyce Bassett
Mike Goodwin
Gary Hahn

ART DIRECTOR
Carin Lane

MAP ILLUSTRATIONS
Jeff Boyer

RESEARCH DIRECTOR
Sarah Hinman Ryan

COPY EDITORS
Alan Abair
Teresa Buckley
Steve Cheslow
Bill Federman
James R. Gray
Mike Jarboe
Susan Mehalick
Tracy Ormsbee
Daniel Roberts
John Runfola
Joe Stalvey
Lisa Morey Stevens
Toni Toczlowski

SYSTEM SUPPORT
Sandi Costello
Jim White

ONLINE PRODUCERS
Paul Block
Trudi Shaffer

ON THE WEB
To see more stories and photos, watch videos and
purchase additional copies of this book:

http://timesunion.com/albanyrural

AUTHOR'S NOTE ON SOURCES

PHOTOS & ILLUSTRATIONS:
Page 21: James Hall, (John M. Clarke, "James Hall of Albany: Geologist and Paleontologist. 1811-1898," Albany, N.Y., 1923).

Page 23: Harmanus Bleecker (Harriet Langdon Pruyn Rice, "Harmanus Bleecker: an Albany Dutchman, 1779-1849," William Boyd Printing Company Inc., 1924)

Page 25: Joel Munsell, (Howell Tenney, "History of the County of Albany, N.Y., From 1609 to 1886," New York: W.W. Munsell & Co. Publishers, 1886).

Page 26: An advertisement for Charles Munsell, General Book Binder in The Albany Handbook, compiled by H.P. Phelps (Albany, N.Y.: Brandow & Barton, 1884).

Page 27: Catharine Hamilton's vine-covered tomb (circa 1940), courtesy of the Hamilton family.

Page 31: Illustration of Edward C. Delavan (from article Edward C. Delavan, The Eminent Temperance Advocate, Phrenological Journal, April 1871 issue, p. 234).

Page 32: Delavan House photo and illustration, undated, Times Union archive.

Page 33: Dyer Lathrop, (from Howell Tenney, "History of the County of Albany, N.Y., From 1609 to 1886" New York: W.W. Munsell & Co. Publishers, 1886, page 576.)

Page 35: Learned Hand, courtesy TAUNY, "W is for the Woods."

Page 37: Portrait of John Alden Dix (New York State Capitol, Hall of Governors, painter: Kenneth Frazier).

Page 39: James Bentley "Cy" Seymour, 1909-1911 T206 White Border tobacco card produced by the American Tobacco Trust. From "The T206 Collection: The Players & Their Stories" by Tom and Ellen Zappala.

Page 40: Jack McAuliffe, (from Dictionary of American Portraits, New York: Dover, 1967, page 397.)

Page 41: 1893 N266 Red Cross Tobacoo Ryan/McAuliffe Boxing card. (SGC)

Page 42: William James, Ezra Ames, 1822, oil on canvas. Courtesy Union College Permanent Collection.

Page 44: A photograph of Marcus T. Reynolds (circa 1897), Albany Institute of History & Art Library, a gift from the Fort Orange Club Archives. Photographer unknown.

Page 50: RMS Titanic (April 10, 1912), black-and-white photograph, Associated Press.

Page 54: Chester A. Arthur, President of the United States (1882), Library of Congress, (photographer: C.M. Bell)

Page 60: Photograph of Albany Almshouse Jan. 18, 1932, Times Union archive.

Page 61: Etching of the former Albany Academy building designed by architect Philip J. Hooker in Albany, N.Y., undated. Times Union archive.

Page 63: Volkert Petrus Douw (1720-1891), Albany Chronicles: A History of the City Arranged Chronologically, Compiled by Cuyler Reynolds, [J.B. Lyon Company, Printers, 1906], page 368.

Page 64: John V.L Pruyn, (Amasa J. Parker, "Landmarks of Albany County") (1897).

Page 68: Edwin T. "Ebby" Thacher, Courtesy of the Thacher Family.

Page 69: Bookjacket of "Ebby: The Man Who Sponsored Bill W," by Mel B. (Amazon)

Page 70: Andrew Meneely and sample bell, courtesy of Dan Meneely.

Page 72: Advertisements from a page of the 1845 Albany City Directory for Schuyler & Co.'s Old Line Tow Boats, Captain "Commander" Samuel Schuyler's steamer Rip Van Winkle and Samuel's son James' coal business.

Page 74: Illustration of Henry Burden (from his daughter Margaret Burden Proudfit's, Henry Burden: His Life and a history of his inventions compiled from the public press [Troy, N.Y.: Pafraets

Press, 1904], page 48.

Page 76: Portrait believed to be Anneke Jantz Bogardus, Mrs. Mary Helen (Robert H. Ruinton) of Morriston, Fla., (painter: unknown, photographer: Robert Trask II) (from William Brower Bogardus, Dear Cousin: A Charted Genealogy of the Descendants of Anneke Jans Bogardus (1605-1663) to the 5th Generation, 1996)

Page 77: Portrait of Domine Everardus Bogardus, (painter: unknown, photograph courtesy of New York State Parks, Recreation and Historic Preservation, Senate House State Historic Site) (from William Brower Bogardus, Dear Cousin: A Charted Genealogy of the Descendants of Anneke Jans Bogardus (1605-1663) to the 5th Generation, 1996)

Page 78: Patroness Bandina Bleecker Dudley (seated, lower left) in a painting of the Dudley Observatory Dedication (1857), Albany Institute of History & Art Library, gift from Gen. Amasa J. Parker , (painter: Tompkins H. Matteson).

Page 79: A 1857 painting of the Dudley Observatory dedication by Tompkins H. Matteson that hangs at the Albany Institute of History & Art.

Page 80: William Learned Marcy (between 1855-1865), Library of Congress, (photographers: Brady-Handy Photograph Collection).

Page 82: Newspaper clip, An Awful Fatality – One Lady Killed and Another Seriously Injured – The Rural Cemetery the Scene of the Tragedy, The Troy Times, Saturday, June 2, 1877.

Page 84: John Flack Winslow. Historical and Genealogical Record, Dutchess and Putnam counties, New York, 1912. Library of Congress.

Page 85: USS Monitor at the Battle of Hampton Roads. Associated Press.

Page 91: Stephen Van Rensselaer III, photographic reprint of an original pastel portrait, Rensselaer Polytechnic Institute Department of Institute Archives and Special Collections

Page 93: Charles Hoy Fort, Courtesy the Spain family.

Page 97: Willard W. Glazier, Down the Great River: Embracing an account of the Discovery of the true source of the Mississippi, [Hubbard Brothers Publishers, 1889], frontispiece)

Page 98: Willard W. Glazier, the book cover from "Sword and Pen," by Willard Glazier and an illustration of Glazier from his book "Headwaters of the Mississippi. Library of Congress

Page 99: Josiah Goodrich Root, Landmarks of Albany County by Amasa J. Parker (1897).

Page 100: Major General Philip Schuyler. From Dictionary of American Portraits, New York: Dover, 1967.

Page 103: The Indian Ladder Trail at Thacher State Park in Voorheesville, N.Y. (Lori Van Buren/Times Union)

Page 104: John G. Myers, (from New York State Men: Biographic Studies and Character Portraits, compiled and edited by Frederick S. Hills (The Argus Company, 1910).

Page 105: The John G. Myers Store collapse. Times Union archive

Page 106: Edwin Corning, father of Mayor Erastus Corning 2nd (1926), Courtesy Wharton Sinkler III)

Page 107: Albany Mayor Erastus Corning 2nd speaks before a crowd on June 13, 1949. (Times Union Archive)

Page 109: A hand-colored lithograph postcard from the early 1900s of the Angel at the Sepulchre, purchased by collector Barb Casey, a volunteer at the Albany Institute of History & Art. (Barb Casey collection)

Page 110: Carte De Visit of Erastus Dow Palmer, Albany Institute of History & Art, (artist: unknown).

Page 112: Photo of Brevet Maj. Charles E. Pease, courtesy of Mark Bodnar.

Page 113: The room in the McLean House, at Appomattox where Gen. Lee surrendered to Gen. Grant, undated, Library of Congress .

Page 113: Gen. Ulysses S. Grant, between 1860 and 1870, Library of Congress.

Page 113: Gen. Robert E. Lee, March 1864 Library of Congress . (Julian Vannerson, photographer).

Page 114: Portrait of artist Charles Calverley (1864), Albany Institute of History & Art Library (a gift from Elizabeth E. Baker) , (painter: Elliott Charles Loring).

Page 116: Thurlow Weed (1797-1882), Library of Congress, (artist: unknown.)

Page 118: Peter Kinnear, (from Howell Tenney, History of the County of Albany, N.Y., From 1609 to 1886 [New York: W.W. Munsell & Co. Publishers, 1886], page 597.

Page 119: Inventor John Wesley Hyatt of the Albany Billiard Ball Company, undated. (Albany County Historical Association's Hall of Fame/Times Union archive). Charlotte Stadler working at the Albany Billiard Ball Company, Jan., 1978, in Albany, N.Y. (Bob Richey/Times Union archive)

BOOKS:
Churchill, Henry W. Churchill's "Guide through the Albany Rural Cemetery." Albany: Churchill, 1857.

Fitzgerald, Edward. "A Hand Book for the Albany Rural Cemetery." Albany: Van Benthuysen Printing House, 1871.

Greene, Meg. "Rest in Peace: A History of American Cemeteries." Minneapolis: Twenty-First Century Books, 2008.

Grondahl, Paul. "Mayor Corning: Albany Icon, Albany Enigma." Albany: Washington Park Press, 1997.

Hess, Peter J. "People of Albany: During Albany's Second 200 Years (1800s & 1900s)." Albany: Albany Rural Cemetery, 2007.

Hess, Peter J. "Who Were the People of Albany? Interesting and Important People, Albany Rural Cemetery." Albany: Albany Rural Cemetery, 2008.

Hess, Peter J. "People of Albany and the Civil War." Albany: Albany Rural Cemetery, 2008.

Johnson, Eugene J. "Style Follows Function: Architecture of Marcus T. Reynolds." Albany: Washington Park Press and Mount Ida Press, 1993.

Kennedy, William. "O Albany!: Improbable City of Political Wizards, Fearless Ethnics, Spectacular Aristocrats, Splendid Nobodies, and Underrated Scoundrels." New York: The Viking Press and Washington Park Press, 1983.

McEneny, John J. "Albany: Capital City on the Hudson." Albany: Windsor Publications, 1981.

Phelps, Henry P. "The Albany Rural Cemetery: Its Beauties, Its Memories." Albany: Phelps and Kellogg, 1893.

Waite, Diana S., editor. "Architects in Albany." Albany: Mount Ida Press & Historic Albany Foundation, 2009.

WEBSITES:
Albany Institute of History and Art. http://www.albanyinstitute.org/

Albany Rural Cemetery blog. http://albanyruralcemetery.blogspot.com/

Albany Rural Cemetery digitized burial cards. http://www.ancestry.com

Find a Grave. http://www.findagrave.com/

Library of Congress. http://www.loc.gov

New York State Museum. http://www.nysm.nysed.gov

New York Times archives. http://www.nytimes.com

Online Archives of California. http://www.oac.cdlib.org/

Rensselaer Polytechnic Institute archives. http://archives.rpi.edu/

Stanford University archives. http://library.stanford.edu/spc

The Colonial Albany Social History Project. http://www.nysm.nysed.gov/albany/whoarewe.html

Times Union archives. http://www.timesunion.com

U.S. Department of Veterans Affairs. www.cem.va.gov

Williams College archives. http://archives.williams.edu

EXTENDED INTERVIEWS & TOURS

STEFAN BIELINSKI
Retired State Museum social historian Stefan Bielinski is the founder of the Colonial Albany Social History Project and his knowledge of Colonial-era people buried in Albany Rural Cemetery is unsurpassed. His tour of the family plot of Capt. Samuel Schuyler and the so-called "black Schuylers" of early Albany, as well as slaves buried in the Church Grounds, was riveting.

MARK BODNAR
Mark Bodnar is the acknowledged expert on Civil War soldiers and sailors buried in Albany Rural Cemetery and he has identified 1,030 Civil War veterans after 20 years of research. He is at work on a book about the subject and his animated tour of the graves of two of his favorites, Brevet Maj. Charles E. Pease and Lt. William H. Pohlmann, was revelatory.

BILL BRUCE
Bill Bruce is a cemetery trustee and former president of the board whose love affair with Albany Rural began as a teenager when he worked on the summer grounds crew. He brings his family to enjoy the scenic beauty and walks his boxer, Daisy, on the grounds. His spirited tour of the Archibald McIntyre family plot and the monuments of notable Scots underscored his abiding affinity for his Scottish roots.

JOHN BUSZTA
John Buszta is the general manager at Albany Rural Cemetery, where he has worked since 1979. He has an extraordinary command of the cemetery's archives and records that date from its 1841 incorporation. His tour of favorite monuments, including explorer and author Willard Glazier, Cohoes textile titan Josiah Goodrich Root and baseball great James Bentley "Cy" Seymour were highly informative.

PETER HESS
Peter Hess published three books that documented the notable and interesting people buried in Albany Rural Cemetery. He also served as president of the cemetery's board of trustees and wrote dozens of historical articles for the cemetery's newsletter. His prodigious research proved indispensable and he also led an instructive tour of a few favorite plots, including those of Robert Yates and the James family.

MICHAEL HUXLEY
Trustee Michael Huxley is the leading expert on Albany Rural Cemetery's stone carvers and he has tracked the monumental work of these forgotten artisans through more than 100 other cemeteries. His 15-year obsession grew out of daily walks with his dog, Archie, a terrier mix, and the late Gregan, a Jack Russell terrier. His droll commentary and tour of the James Flack Winslow mausoleum, the David Strain monument and others were captivating.

JOHN PIPKIN
John Pipkin is a cemetery trustee and University at Albany professor who specializes in urbanism. He provided key insight into the broader context of the rural cemetery movement. His two-hour conversation with Norman Rice as they sat on a bench along Millionaires' Row in the raking light just before dusk amounted to a graduate course in Albany history.

MICHAEL & LYNN RADLICK
Michael and Lynn Radlick have been jogging, researching and photographing Albany Rural Cemetery for the past 20 years. He is a cemetery trustee and a noted authority on Albany Rural's designer, David Bates Douglass. The couple led a stirring sunrise running tour and an astonishing tramp past long-lost architectural relics hidden in forgotten ravines. Their fervor for the cemetery's natural beauty was infectious.

NORMAN RICE
Norman Rice is the longest-tenured cemetery trustee and a leading authority on the biographies of famous people buried there, particularly artists and architects. His tours of his favorite Middle Ridge area and lively commentary on the Corning family plot, President Chester Arthur, the John Boyd Thacher mausoleum and Marcus T. Reynolds were a source of delight and detailed information. Rice's enthusiasm for the cemetery has inspired many to delve into research at Albany Rural.

INDEX